BREAKFAST
WITH
KINGS

Doron Maman

BREAKFAST WITH KINGS

Doron Maman

Interior Design: Equire Technologies
Cover Design: Doron Maman

ISBN: 978-1-5136-3024-3

International distributor: www.doronmaman.com
Bwk.doron@gmail.com
Tel: +972-50-222-1591
Facebook: Doron Maman
Instagram: breakfast_with_kings

Although we may have not yet met, this book is dedicated to you.
To the person you are today and the royalty you are going
to become tomorrow.

ACKNOWLEDGEMENTS

The writing of 'Breakfast with Kings' would not have been possible without the assistance of some very influential and inspirational individuals.

I have been gifted to be guided by two wonderful mentors, Benny Mevorach and Liat Yanai. Your enthusiasm and willingness to offer your honest insight has truly humbled me and I am genuinely grateful for your time.

Words cannot convey my appreciation for my family and the endless gifts they continuously provide me. You are each my personal reminder that life is a never ending-learning experience.

To my wife Dani: no words can reflect how grateful I am for your patience and support for each of my new and wild endeavors. You are without a doubt my greatest gift and my greatest teacher. I thank you for your relentlessness to drive me towards success.

Lastly, to the original four Kings, this book and philosophy was inspired by each of you. The values, the insights and the collective wisdom you each share has driven me to endlessly explore and recognize the unrecognized Kings and Queens of our world. This book is in honor of them.

I love you all.

"If I have seen further it is not because I am taller, but rather because I have stood on the shoulders of giants."

-SIR ISAAC NEWTON (1676)

CONTENTS

CONTENTS

BREAKFAST

WITH

KINGS

MY FUNERAL

"When you were born, you were crying and everyone else was smiling. Live your life so at the end, you're the one who is smiling and everyone else is crying."
-RALPH WALDO EMERSON

The human body, if provided with water, cannot last longer than thirty days without food. Subsequently, it cannot last longer than three days without water alone. After learning these facts, the question I was left asking was, "How often must we rehydrate the spirit before it begins to sustain damage?" We have become so focused with filling our bodies with food, our technological devices with Wi-Fi and answering our basic needs with external materials, I fear we may have left our interiors hollow and empty. Even the world's most expensive and valuable car will not be able to take you to your destination until you fill it with gas. If this is the case, then why are we not focused on consistently nurturing and refueling our spirits?

Today, more than any time in human history, we are absorbed within a matrix, a fast-paced world dominated by technological devices that have practically dismantled our ability to think and properly communicate with one another. Who needs to give a friend a hug when you can just give him a 'like' on social media, right? And if your post gets shared, that person must really care about you! Just look at our online culture. You will find more pictures of people with their colorful plate of food than pictures of them actually eating it. You may not notice it, but our digestive system is undergoing a transformational process, which now starts with the eyes rather than the stomach. *#Tasty!* We have substituted our basic ability to recognize, encourage, appreciate and love others with a tiny digital box that dictates our daily actions with chiming bells and whistles. Ultimately, the underlying message we radiate to ourselves and the world is simple - as long as we answer our physiological, social and material needs, we will be all right.

It was at this point in my life that I was confronted with a question that radically changed the landscape of my thought process. This reality-shattering, groundbreaking question would change my character forever. "***Who will cry at my funeral?***" Being only twenty years old at the time and in the middle of my mandatory military service, I thought, *I'm young and currently in the most vital years of my life! Why the hell should I be thinking about death?* However, the more I thought about it, the more I understood that age is an irrelevant premise of the argument, as the only guarantee in life is that we are each granted a limited amount of time. Whereas the carton of milk at least has an expiry date, we will never know when to expect our demise. We were not designed to live forever, nor were we ever meant to know when our curtain will fall.

This existentialist mindset can be a terrifying one, but when properly directed it can be genuinely powerful, having a meaningful impact on how we live our lives. In my case, I found myself vividly imagining my burial ceremony if I were to die at that very moment. I saw loved ones standing by my grave being whole-heartedly consoled by friends and estranged characters who I have touched along the way. I heard a combination of laughter with tears, while my friends recalled our timeline of memories. I even heard the voices of faces I did not recognize asking themselves, "What kind of man was he?"

I recommend you try and do the same. Create a vivid image or even an extremely detailed movie of what your funeral would be like if you were to pass at this moment. As you gaze upon the ceremony, try and observe: Who has arrived? What is the expression on the faces of the attendants? Were you surprised by the presence of someone you did not expect? Listen carefully. What are people saying about you? What memories do they share about your time in this world? How do they define your impact and influence? Is your absence now felt? Most importantly, what value are they embracing from your life, to carry on and to apply in their own?

This process can be a truly scary one and I applaud you if you had the guts to mentally envision it. But if you think about it, your funeral is possibly the most fascinating event of your existence. People from all walks of life come to pay their final respects as you are gloriously placed upon your own personal monument. Family members, friends and distant guests come to share and recognize the impact of your presence on the world before your final departure.

Yet there is a brilliant irony to this "once in a lifetime" occasion. That at your grandest of stages, in which you are the sole focus of attention and are enshrined upon a dazzling pedestal of perfection, you are the only person who is not fully present. This notion reveals that despite the show we display to the world, there is a hidden and somewhat dormant humility within each of us of which we are not aware. This pushes us to become more influential and important in our daily lives through our actions. Subsequently, we sincerely hope that these actions will bring others to recognize that we were a part of their lives and a part of this world.

If your mental funeral was anything like mine, then after sincere reflection, your key discovery will be that the quality of your life is in direct correlation with the quality of your relationships. The more meaningful, impactful and influential our relationships are, the greater our experiences in life. It is about how we have affected others and had our lives affected by them. Thomas Campbell brought this concept to life when he so brilliantly said, "To live in hearts we leave behind is not to die." We continue to live in this world by investing pieces of our character in others.

Humbly serving friends, family, and strangers, in ways only we know how, allows us to authentically deliver our personal, fingerprint-like essence to all that we touch. With each person we impact, we gain another potential participant for our funeral and further signify our impression on this world. This further fossilizes our values, which hopefully will contribute for future generations to come. But even more importantly, by doing this, we create a platform for others to recognize their essence and help establish their unique contribution to the world.

These notions of our immortality and their effects on who we are as individuals have been deeply researched in the world of psychology under the title of Terror Management Theory (1973). The principal message being that we are consistently reminded of our mortality in everyday life, and when we are, we search for ways to become of value in order to comfort this notion. We fully pursue opportunities to become more meaningful and influential as we understand that it is then that our spirits are fully replenished. It is imperative for us to absorb the fact that no external device can do what a single meaningful face-to-face conversation or experience can. These are the moments when we successfully exit the matrix! With all that, I return to my initially proposed question, "How often must we rehydrate our spirits before we endure damage?" In the direction we are currently going, it is almost as if we have been engaging in a prolonged fast of value, losing sight of our well that can replenish our spirits by connecting with others. I was ready to **break** this *fast* in a consistent manner, which would fill me with all the possible sources of meaning and value.

The only question now was, "Who do I invite to breakfast?"

Long Live the Kings and Queens!

With more than seven and a half billion anatomically alike creatures on this planet, we are each miraculously the only of our kind. Each one of us has experienced specific events that only occurred to us, events resulting in understandings that only we comprehend, which affect and direct our behavior in a manner that can only be displayed by us. Considering this process happens to each of us on a daily basis, the growing and learning opportunities are infinite! This leads us to the development of a unique fingerprint-like essence, which is actually our gift that we contribute to the world. Just as a majestic King or Queen rules justly over their land, they must watch over their citizens and provide them with whatever is needed to live and thrive. Discovering and providing our essence for others does exactly that.

This philosophy provided me with two profoundly important findings:

I.   All the characters in my life have an essence and value to contribute. Therefore, I must accept what they have to give.
II. I have an essence and value to contribute to this world. Therefore, I must strive to deliver it to others.

The application of our essence through our actions empowers others with the values that we have to provide, while simultaneously creating a platform in which they can contribute their core principles to the world. I have dubbed these individuals, "Kings and Queens," as I feel that this is the respect that we each deserve when willing to give our heart whilst humbly learning from others. By frequently congregating with such royalty and taking the time to learn from them, comes the marvelous opportunity to humbly strengthen ourselves, our core values and our potentially eternal presence in the world.

It is important for me to stress to you, the reader, that although I define these individuals as royalty, they are no more unique than any individual you have encountered in your life (including and especially yourself). We are all growing Queens and Kings with the power of contribution. I mean everyone, from the most powerful CEO to the janitor in your workplace - they are all gifted with a unique seed of royalty. However, the development of this attribute is a lifetime process that requires patience, persistence and sincere humility.

Of these requirements, humility plays a key role as we do not know if and when others are watching us or being influenced by our actions. Therefore, we must be consistently committed to sharing our essence with any person we come into contact with. This humbleness is only further established when we strive to learn from the Kings and Queens in our lives, bringing everybody around us to a more royal level. As John F. Kennedy once so meticulously said, "A rising tide lifts all boats." This is the process of becoming that tide in your life.

In this book, I have dedicated ten chapters in honor of different Kings and Queens who have influentially affected my life, ultimately pushing me to impact the lives of others (including you). These memoirs tell stories of our shared adventures and are then followed by three valuable life lessons which they have provided me (knowingly and unknowingly). However, beyond my desire to connect you to my newly gained appreciations, the true power of this book lies in your willingness for implementation. Each value section is concluded with several mentally engaging questions that will challenge you to bring this knowledge to a royal level of wisdom. As a fellow caring human being, I personally recommend that you keep a journal and take the time to answer these questions genuinely. The journey of self-exploration begins by searching for answers from within, and this can be your chance to become royal!

As I began my search for these highnesses, I started looking throughout my life for protagonists and heroes who radiated inspiring characteristics: integrity, determination, industriousness, passion, hunger for success, resilience, competitive greatness, love, humility, endless learning, out of the box thinking, charisma and so much more. I am talking about the kind of people who do not fear their own capabilities or the circumstances they face that they cannot change. They graciously smile in the face of adversity and confront it with their own distinct approach knowing they will arise victorious. These wise characters passionately challenge their essence to further discover their potential contribution, thereby widening the foundation of their kingdom.

This book contains just a few of my adventures with the hidden treasures of the world and the lessons I have captured from them in order to become a greater King. I humbly dedicate this book to you with great love and respect, as you too now embark on your epic journey towards royalty.

Royal Food for Thought

- If you were to pass away at this very moment, what would your funeral look like? What legacy are you currently leaving in this world?
- What characteristics will you search for in your quest of discovering Kings and Queens?
- What value do you wish to emulate as a King or Queen?

1

TWO ICE CUBES AND THE HIPPIE

"If you really want to do something, you'll find a way. If you don't, you'll find an excuse."

-JIM ROHN

"Welcome to high school. I shifted from a whale in a pond to an anchovy in an ocean. Special treatment was no longer an option and it was time to man up (not as I did at my Bar Mitzvah). I stepped onto a campus of more than thirty-five hundred students. I was a young, chubby freshman, lost and in need of an on-campus GPS to find out which way to go and who I could trust. I inspected my class schedule to discover my first class of the week was a mandatory course called "Health."

Ironically, I was not a healthy individual. Growing up as a kid, I was always the 'big boy' of the class. Always the one picked after the girls during PE because I was too slow. Always trying to get the junk food from the top shelves of the snack room or the other kids' lunch boxes. I just loved to eat. In fact, according to my parents, within the first twenty-four hours following my birth, the nurses approached them and claimed that they could no longer provide me with baby formula because I was eating three times more than all the other infants. Until my mother's release, my parents were asked to purchase their own formula separately.

I explored the campus looking for the classroom, until I found more freshmen standing around a busted old caravan behind the school parking lot. I had found my new classroom. Inside, the caravan was filled with old posters of anti-smoking campaigns from the early eighties, various safe-sex references and cute pictures of cats grabbing on to tree branches with the words "Hang in there!" written across the bottom. As I sat in the class with my new classmates observing the exhibition of vintage posters, the door surprisingly slammed. "Good morning students, my name is Robert Cooper, but you can call me Rob. I'll be teaching this class!" Rob was a tall fit man with grey curly hair. He almost always came dressed wearing a pair of jeans and a tucked-in, buttoned-down Hawaiian shirt. He was one of those guys who refused to apply deodorant because he believed the body should always be breathing freely. The curls in his hair would spring wildly as he would energetically bounce around the class with his retro hippie vibe. But most importantly, he was the kind of teacher that you could always sense had true wisdom that exceeded the borders of the classroom.

It immediately became evident that Rob was not your average teacher. Throughout the semester, Rob would educate us on everything that the average parent would hope to never discuss with their kids. Yet Rob was a pro and would never let you feel weird about these subjects. He would just laugh it off, saying something like, "That's just how your body works and that's okay."

Halfway through the semester, Rob brought in a Body Mass Index (BMI) specialist to give us a better understanding of our personal health. If you are not familiar with this measurement, this checks if your weight is in proportion to your height. Based on the score received, you can compare it to a chart to see if you are in the proper weight class or are in need of a change to get in the right shape. Rob told us that today's class would be dedicated to measuring our BMI, so we can further understand our bodies. The students dispersed into small groups as we were each called up to the scale one by one. As I stepped up, I could feel the machine judging me, making its calculations until it printed a small piece of paper with a number on it. Twenty-nine. It did not really mean anything to me; all I really knew was that it was after twenty-eight and before thirty. *Whatever*, I thought.

Finally, the bell rang, which meant it was my favorite time of the day, lunch! As we all sprinted for the door, Rob wished us all a great day and finished with saying, "Doron, can you please stay for just one minute?"

My classmates rushed for the quad to get in line for the delicious pre-made bean and cheese burritos, as I immediately began to assess my behavior during the class. *Did I do something wrong?*

The door shut behind the last student as Rob sat me down. Then in the most straight-forward manner, he looked me in the eye and dropped the bomb on me. "I'm worried about you, kid. You got a twenty-nine. You may not understand what that means, but that's bad. By bad, I mean really bad. You're already on the verge of obesity."

I suddenly heard my own voice yelling inside of my head. *Me, obese! What are you talking about? I like to eat, but I'm not obese!*

Rob recognized my thought process and continued. "But don't worry. You're actually quite lucky. You're in a place in your life where you can still make a change. I suggest that change be joining a sports team. Effective immediately!"

Still bewildered by what I was just told, not being able to digest this new information, I asked, "What do you suggest?"

He grinned and replied, "Wrestling."

At my high school, wrestling was recognized as the most badass sport to be a part of. Beyond the necessary aggressiveness and mental toughness, we were talking about three-per-day practices: one hour of weighted sled sprints before school, one and a half hours of lifting weights during school (instead of PE) and three hours of wrestling after school. The concept of working out was beyond me as I was still unable to do a single pushup! I seemed to only go down and never had the strength to push myself back up. As intense as all that sounded, the only thought more petrifying than those practices was the thought of me being an obese individual. It was time for a change.

I started to train, driving myself harder than ever before. I still was not the most aggressive person, but I was a man on a mission. To lose weight and get healthy! I took a lot of heat from the team, as I was the big guy who was weak and slow. Matters did not get any better when I lost to one of the girls on the team who weighed thirty pounds less than me. Although I was the easy target, I refused to be broken.

After a couple months of hard work, I was shedding weight and feeling good, until one Friday afternoon, I was approached by the coach and a fellow teammate from a lower weight category. The coach placed a hand on our shoulders and pulled us in for a talk. "All right boys, tomorrow is the tournament. Doron, you and Curtis are going to be switching weight classes because we think Curtis will have a better chance in your division. So for tomorrow's tournament, we need you to go down from one hundred and fifty-six pounds to one hundred forty-seven pounds. Curtis, you good with that?"

What? I screamed inside of my head.

"Yeah coach, I'm game." Curtis joyously responded. He was a state-ranked wrestler with a winners' mindset, so of course he was game. At that point, both sets of eyes locked on to me. "Doron?"

In doubt of any chance of success, I looked at the coach and responded, "Just to make sure we are all on the same page. You want me to drop about nine pounds in sixteen hours?" I was not even sure if it was physically possible.

With his hands now on his hips, the coach confidently responded, "That's right."

I did not have much of a choice. I looked within for any untapped sources of strength and said aloud in disbelief, "All right. Let's get to work!" According to the coach, it was simple (yet torturous): all I had to do was to perform three hours of sprints and an hour of wrestling. I got dressed with my hooded sweatshirt and sweat pants, with a trash bag over my torso, beanie on my head then closed the hoodie of the sweatshirt over that, allowing me to secrete more fluids from my body. Of course, there were several additional guidelines. For example, I could not eat until the weigh in, because food is equivalent to extra weight. I could not drink either, because water is also weight. Therefore, my only dietary intake for that sixteen-hour period would be two exceptionally delicious frozen ice cubes. Only after I would weigh in, and hopefully make weight, I would be able to feast on whatever I wished.

Those were the longest four hours of my life, but I sucked it up and made it through. I came home to enjoy my delectable serving of two ice cubes, sluggishly crawled into bed and said a final prayer to reach my goal. Coach told me I would lose about two pounds in my sleep, so I started feeling hopeful.

At the crack of dawn, I was up on my fragile feet and on my way to the tournament. My game face was on, despite physical exhaustion and the general anxiety of whether I would make the weight or not. The weigh-ins were held in the school gymnasium. Each wrestler would get on a stage where all two hundred and fifty participants, friends and family could see, as the referees would make sure each wrestler did not exceed the allotted weight. I had to be one hundred and forty-seven pounds on the dot. A single ounce more would disqualify my participation automatically, forfeiting potential points for my team. I waited anxiously until my name was finally called. I climbed the stairs to the stage and placed myself before the scale. My heart pounded thunderously through my chest as I exhaled deeply and stepped up onto the digital weight. The numbers recklessly danced up and down, as the scale conducted its calculations. I shut my eyes, waiting for the referee to call my weight aloud. "One hundred forty-seven point four pounds!"

No way! I screamed at myself in my head. *After all of that, I won't be able to participate because of a fraction of a pound!* Coach effortlessly read my thoughts through my body language and immediately intervened. "Don't worry Doron. You have an additional thirty minutes to try and drop the remaining weight." He suggested that I try to excrete anything I could in the bathroom. I then suggested that I had nothing in my body except for two stupid ice cubes!

For those thirty minutes I ran, skipped rope, did crunches and anything else I could to diminish the invisible weight. Despite running on an empty tank, I pushed myself even further. I prayed that maybe there would be a surprise and that God would not let me down after having come so far.

As the time expired, I approached the stage once again. In what felt similar to the climax of a Hollywood film, I placed myself upon the scale. This was the moment of truth! As the digital numbers carelessly fluctuated up and down, I closed my eyes, praying for God to meet me halfway. But yet again, the referee would break my heart calling aloud, "One hundred forty-seven point three pounds! "

Before becoming doused with anger, I reflected on a single question. "Did I do everything in my power to reach success?"

The answer was no, as a new solution dawned upon me. I suddenly grinned while looking at my coach. "We've come this far. To hell with it." I took off my briefs and stood as naked as the day I was born in front of two hundred and fifty school mates and teachers, praying that the removal of my underpants might give me the final edge. As a single camera flashed and flirtatious whistles echoed from the audience, the referee called aloud, "One forty-six point nine! He's good to go!"

I jumped with joy as the crowd applauded only after putting on my tighty-whities. I probably should have done so in the opposite order. But then, with the adrenaline pumping fiercely through my veins and a new-found ferociousness in my blood, I was ready to take on an entire army of world-class wrestlers. No obstacle could stand in my way. I was walking tall and feeling strong as I fearlessly faced my opponent in the center of the mat. I had the eye of the tiger. I looked him dead in the eye with a look that said, "You have no chance! Bring it on!" The referee blew the whistle, and the next thing I remember was my back being pinned to the floor. The match had concluded and I had suffered a devastating loss in less than twelve seconds. My tournament came to an end.

The season would continue and ultimately I would become the holder of a new school record. I was the only wrestler in the school's history to remain winless the entire season, losing every single match. A record of zero wins and sixteen losses. Yet despite it all, it is this record that I hold with great esteem and pride as amongst my greatest victories to date.

Brutal Loving Honesty

"The truth shall set you free!" However, I sincerely feared to face the fact that I was overweight. I utilized various defense mechanisms and other strategies to overlook the reflection in the mirror and see what was evidently obvious. We all use these mechanisms in our lives, as they help us protect our ego and sense of self. Psychology has recognized different forms of these tactics such as rationalization, denial, dissociation, sublimation, projection and many more. These strategies work effectively, keeping us a distance from that which we fear most about ourselves.

However, the problem is that by allowing these tactics to run their course, we dramatically hinder our potential growth and even endanger our very existence. I mean, is it not funny that people still light up a cigarette despite the presence of a big bolded sentence on the box stating, "This product contains forty-three cancerous substances that can kill you?" Do we not all know that eating refined sugars and fast food is unhealthy and detrimental? But do we stop? Hell no! We find our comfortable ways around it to make sure that not only can we enjoy our guilty pleasure, but we can still love and accept ourselves in the process. We all apply these mechanisms in life, but once we conquer them, we discover meaningful growth.

In retrospect, it is clearly evident that Rob was a great King, who had mastered brutal loving honesty, the bulldozer that shatters defensive walls. What I mean is that in order for us to penetrate our mental barriers, we must get disturbed. As in mad dog, crazy, off the rails disturbed. Something must bother us, pain us and create enough internal cognitive friction that we know that the only viable choice is action. As Edmund Burke put so well, "The only thing necessary for the triumph of evil, is for good men to do nothing." This lack of action is what leads us to participate in such foolish and self-destructive behaviors. We must be strong enough to face the fact that we are doing nothing and then embrace for a change.

Getting disturbed requires one of the two scenarios to occur:

1. Somebody else gets brutally honest with you, placing you in front of your potential consequences.
2. You get brutally honest with yourself and face your potential consequences.

For me, Rob was the first person in my life to slap me (verbally) with the harsh reality that I was going the wrong way. Often times, friends and family wish to protect us and will go to great distances to make sure we do not get hurt. Unknowingly and without intention, our loved ones are actually causing us long-term damage. Rob, being the King he was, approached me like nobody had before, presenting the fact (I was fat), the consequences (I could become obese) and a potential plan of action for change (join the wrestling team). Rob's love for others and his deeply-rooted care for youths is what gave him the confidence to be that person in my life to step up and be brutally lovingly honest. I am forever grateful for his gift.

Royal Food for Thought

- What do you have to be brutally honest about with yourself?
- What defense mechanisms have you set up that you need to hurdle?
- What fact must you face that will disturb you so much that you say, "No more!"?

Make the Choice, Face Yourself

Once you have faced the brutal loving truth, you once again have two possible courses of action. The first is to stay where you are. You have now seen both sides of the coin, and just because the truth is out there does not mean that you must accept it as your own.

Reality is a purely subjective experience and always comes down to a choice of what you decide to see, and only then, what you decide to act on.

The second plan requires that you now become brutally honest with yourself and commit to a plan of action. You know the truth along with the mechanisms and strategies you must apply to remove yourself from it, so what are you going to do about it? This new side must disturb you so much that you become committed to making a change!

How do you know if it disturbs you enough? Simple. Are you pained when you think of the potential consequences? Can you look yourself in the mirror knowing the price you will pay when making that decision? Can you accept how these consequences will affect the people you genuinely love? Ask these questions and you will easily know whether you are disturbed enough or not.

In my case, taking action meant pushing myself beyond my known limits. It meant coming before school for sprints, taking time during school to lift and staying after school to work. It meant working the angles rather than praying for angels. It involved participating in exercises I never had seen before, while igniting muscles I had never used before. The consequences of not taking these steps haunted me with images of what I may have become had Rob not challenged my status.

Rob's honesty propelled me into a state in which I would be changed for the better, forever. Over the last thirteen years, it has instilled within me a healthy life-style culture. I have become a more dynamic and braver man who has the balls to say, "Let's kick ass today," even if the chances of success are slim to none. Today, this belief holds true for all challenges and not only the physical ones. The power to face yourself will allow you to explore your abilities in ways like never before, while recognizing the true power that lies within your core. The choice comes down to this; you can either be your own greatest enemy (becoming a victim to your defense mecha-nisms) or your own greatest ally (doing what's best for you). What will you choose?

Royal Food for Thought

- Which reality are you choosing to see? What are you therefore choosing to act on?
- What daily action are you willing to commit to, in order to get closer to achieving success?

Victory is a State of Mind, Not a Record

What is the true meaning of victory? I was laughed at, pointed at, picked on, beat up and experienced pretty much everything else you can imagine, simply because I never had a single win on paper. But what do you think is harder; winning every match of the season or losing every match yet still showing up tenaciously to fight? Although I may only be able to answer the latter, the personal strength to drag my butt out to the wrestling mat everyday and consistently reestablish within myself the belief that I could win was tough as nails.

Pushing myself mentally to the point that as a fifteen-year-old boy I stood naked in front of two-hundred and fifty people, just to get the chance to fight, was a true moment of victory. It was my way of sur-rendering to God and telling him "Hey man, I've done everything in my power. Please help me the rest of the way as you see fit." Such peace of mind is priceless.

I left the sport of wrestling not only with a winless record, but with an understanding that victory is not measured by the trophies in your office, the records you hold or the accomplishments you have achieved. It is about being tough enough to keep coming back swinging, especially when the odds are stocked against you. Know that life will throw everything at you, including the kitchen sink, and then let us see how you move. Sylvester Stallone put it so well in his film *Rocky Balboa* (2006): "It's not about how hard you can hit. It's about how hard you get hit and keep moving forward, how much you can take and keep moving forward. That's how winning is done!"

If this is our new definition of victory, then take the opportunity to look back at your life and redefine an event that you may have declared as a failure or setback. Did you come back out of the gates hungrier than before? Did you knock your own expectations off their feet? Did you bounce off the floor resiliently, coming back up stronger than before? If your answer is yes for any of these, then this was a clear victory for you, the home team!

Who would have thought that all these understandings happened because a hippie told me I was fat? Beautiful.

Royal Food for Thought

- Define "Victory."
- With regard to your new definition, what event in your life has now shifted from 'failure' to 'victorious'?
- How will this newfound victory serve you upon your next endeavor?

2

WHERE SOCRATES MET BUDDHA

"When you realize how perfect everything is, you will tilt your head back and laugh at the sky."
-FIONA ROBYN

We will be landing in our destination in ten minutes. Please fasten your seat belts and put your chairs in the upright position. Thank you for choosing Thai Airways and enjoy your stay here in Phuket, Thailand." After more than fifteen hours of traveling, I was more than ready to get off the less than half-occupied airplane to begin my new adventure. I was halfway through my bachelor's degree in psychology and without much thought, spontaneously decided to embark on a solo adventure to a destination I knew nothing about, to take part in something I have never done before: Mixed Martial Arts (MMA).

Two weeks earlier, I was at home watching on YouTube old fight clips of Mike Tyson, the former world heavy weight boxing champion. This man was bad. Spectators would observe in awe as he fearlessly stood toe-to-toe in the center of the ring with men twice his size and would then effortlessly tear them apart limb from limb. I became deeply intrigued. Beyond his impetuous style, impregnable defense and ferociousness in the ring, he had a whole process that led to the first chime of the bell signaling the start of the fight. I asked myself, "What's 'mentally' required of a person, to push him or her to such extremes? How does a person develop such confidence that they could stand looking up at such towering modern-day Goliaths, yet still come out throwing vicious punches?" I was captivated and wished to understand the training process and rituals performed to become such an unbreakable competitor (both mentally and physically).

I began to search online and found a MMA training camp located in Phuket, a small island in the Southwest corner of Thailand located in the Andaman Sea, just an hour's flight from Bangkok. The island was divided into three general areas: an urban area for the tourists, an urban area for the locals and the jungle that separated the two. I knew little to nothing about Thailand or MMA, but I knew that if I wanted to discover what it took for Tyson and other fighting greats to get in the ring and rifle punches, I had to take this opportunity. In less than twenty-four hours, I purchased my tickets, booked a room on the training camp and was ready to leave for an experience for which I was not prepared.

The aircraft's wheels touched the sticky Thai ground and I made my way out of the terminal into the heavily humid weather. It was like being repetitively smacked by a moist towel. I began looking for the taxi I ordered online that would take me to the training grounds, but it was nowhere to be found. I stood alone in a small Thai terminal, engulfed in a dense forest. It was getting late and pretty dark outside. I became nervous as I was no longer sweating from just the moist Thai air. I had no idea which way to go or who I could trust. I started asking by-passers and cab drivers how to get to the fighting camp, while pointing at a picture of a logo of the camp. But most of them looked at me and just started yelling words in Thai. After more than forty-five minutes of searching, one cab driver that seemed confident enough told me to get in and that he would take me. I realized I did not have much of a choice, so I jumped in.

As we drove to the location, I started to second guess myself. *Damn! What were you thinking Doron? You're going to let some guy drive you into the middle of the jungle, in the middle of Asia, in the middle of the night?* The more we drove, the further we distanced ourselves from civilization and I was praying to see some familiar sign from the pictures I saw online. A billboard, a banner, anything to let me know I was on the right path.

After almost an hour of driving, we pulled up to the camp. It was definitely the place, but it seemed abandoned. All the lights were off, the boxing rings were empty and an old toothless security guard sat on a foldable metal chair at the entrance fidgeting with his thumbs. I paid the cab, grabbed my gear and approached the guard.

"Hello," I said announcing the syllables slowly. "Where do I check in my bags?"

The old toothless guard broke out into laughter responding, "No English! No English!" I was already regretting the choice I made to travel alone. I was in the center of the Thai jungle and without a place to stay.

Suddenly, a bulky man with legs like tree trunks mysteriously walked in from out of the darkness. Without much to say, he looked me up and down and said, "Come with me."

As he accompanied me onto the grounds, I was still very much on edge, not sure who I was following. All the lights were off as it was past 11:00 P.M., but you could see at least eight boxing rings protected by thin metal huts, an MMA octagon ring and a fully-equipped Cross-Fit training facility consisting of ropes, tires and barbells. This place looked unbelievable, and it was pitch dark! The man walked me to one of the bungalow rooms. "Stay here tonight. Morning take care."

I respectfully bowed my head towards the Mr. Miyagi-like character. "Sawadee kap," I said, which means 'thank you' in Thai. As I entered the room, I turned on the flickering light to find four white walls, a slightly crooked bed and a beat down television that was at least twenty years old. It felt like a kingdom.

After a few hours of sleep, I woke up the following morning to the sound of two women screaming aloud, "Hurry up, the first Muay Thai class is starting!" Muay Thai is Thailand's culturally-renowned sport of kick boxing. Each fighter enters the ring wearing only boxing gloves and is allowed to deliver to their opponent punches, elbows, kicks and knees to almost any part of the body (aside from the groin). In fact, it is said that the Thai knee kick is the deadliest blow that can be delivered with a human body part in physical combat sports.

There was no time to waste. I had to be a part of this. I grabbed my boxing gloves and followed the women to the training ground. Forgetting jet lag, I was wide awake. This was a two-and-a-half-hour session consisting of thirty minutes of barefoot running, Muay Thai techniques, punching bag work, sparring and footwork, and was intermittently divided by about two hundred and fifty push-ups. I was getting pulverized and taking more hits than I was delivering. All I could think was *Is this really the beginner's class?*

To make matters more challenging, you could not understand a word the head trainer would say. He was a small Thai man who wore a bandana and walked around with a thick bamboo stick that he had just picked up that morning from a nearby field. His razor-sharp eyes could cut right through you as he would heavily mumble his instructions. Luckily for us, he moved his body and showed the movements, so all we had to do was copy and paste.

In the final minutes of the class, he stood us all in a line and began to talk. Nobody understood a word he said. As his tone drastically fluctuated through his one-minute explanation, his last sentence became utterly clear. "You mess up, I hit you with stick! Everybody understand me?"

Wait, what did he just say? Suddenly I felt like a soldier back in basic training, yelling along with all the other training cadets at the top of my voice, "Yes sir!"

We started going through the movements. I was more focused now than I was during any of my exams throughout my degree (talk about a new studying technique). Luckily for me, my movements were solid. However, one of the other guys was not so fortunate. The trainer pulled him aside and whipped his butt with that bamboo stick like he was his momma and he had just uttered the foulest of words. The man obviously flinched at first, to which the trainer responded, "Take like boy! Not like ladyboy!" It was pretty funny and, luckily for us, not as bad as we thought.

That day continued with three more CrossFit training sessions, classic boxing and MMA. I was training with people from all corners of the earth and getting educated like never before. Amateur fighters, professional fighters, people who came to lose weight, people who came to gain muscle and everything in between. However, my category of purpose was different. I came to strengthen "mental muscle" and as soon as I began to gain traction, I began to feel at home.

As the final class of the day concluded, my muscles synchronously collapsed. All I wanted to do was sit outside my room with a refreshing beverage, allow my body to recover and jot down my insights from the day in my journal. The humid Thai air had also decided to temporarily retire at that hour and for this I was equally grateful.

After about ten minutes of writing, I suddenly heard a voice, "Excuse me, mate. Got a light?" I looked up and saw this glowing character with the figure of a body builder and an unlit cigarette in his mouth. The light bulb above his bald head reflected the light back into my eyes. He had a thick Australian accent that sounded like Crocodile Dundee, which seemed funny as he visually appeared to be more like Popeye.

"Sorry man, I don't," I replied.

"Are you the bloke next door to me here? Nice to meet you, mate. My name is Sok."

"Hey man, nice to meet you. I'm Doron." As I replied, I thought to myself, *What kind of name is Sok? Does he 'sok' people, like punch them? Do the letters stand for something?* "I've never heard that name, where are you from?"

"I'm from down under. The name is actually short for Socrates. I live in Australia but my family is Greek."

As his name indicated, Sok was truly a unique thinker and philosopher. That night, we spoke for almost four hours about sports, religion, women, politics and even our perspectives on the meaning of life. Never had I met someone who was so open and trusting of others. He radiated a powerful vibe reflecting his core belief, that there is always good to be found in others. Not the kind of character I expected to meet in a fight camp.

It was evident to me that I had met someone special. I wanted to get to know this man beyond his words. "So Sok, tomorrow morning there is this thing called the Big Buddha Run instead of the CrossFit class. Apparently, there is a mountain in the area where there's a huge Buddha statue at its top. It's something like a three mile climb to the peak. Want to join?"

Sok broke out into his authentic Buddha-like laughter with his head tilted back as he tried to hold his fourth cigarette of the night in his mouth. "You're crazy man, do you know that? I haven't run in only God knows how long…" His laughter turned into a sigh. "Bloody hell mate. Screw it! I'm in! But if I die, you've got to come save me. Deal?" We shook hands and parted to bed.

We woke up several hours later to a drizzling foggy morning and drove out to the base of the Big Buddha Mountain. There were twenty participating athletes and all we could see was a thin road surrounded by a densely green forest, climbing upwards at a forty-degree angle into a thick cloud. The instructor organized the runners at the base.

"It's a race to the top. When you get to Big Buddha, you're done." All that went through my mind was that this was going to be fun. "Ready?" I gave Sok a high five. "Set…" exhaled deeply. "Go!"

The race began and before I knew it I was in the top three competing for the lead. The thickness of the fog did not allow me to see more than twenty feet ahead, so I remained completely committed to what was in front of me. Sok was nowhere in sight, but I was sure he was fine. As we ascended the mountain, we cut through clouds while pushing ourselves for the top position. I suddenly found myself in first. I kicked myself into fifth gear, turned on the nitro and boosted my way to the top. I found myself at the feet of the largest Buddha statue I had ever seen, which stood approximately one hundred and fifty feet tall. The view was out of this world, and the feeling of success was beyond exhilarating, but something was missing. "Sok!"

I turned my back to the peak and began to fly down the mountain, trying not to damage my knees, which were absorbing all the pressure. As I began passing the other climbing fighters, they seemed confused as to why I was descending. About halfway down, I recognized Sok huffing and puffing as if he was getting ready to blow down the brick house of the three little pigs. He was waging a personal war of whether to continue or not, with his gaze buried in the road ahead. I pulled up to him and forcefully removed his backpack off from his back. I placed it on myself and told him, "A deal is a deal. Grab on to the bag." Sok grabbed on for dear life, and together we fought our way to the top. I tried to engage him in conversation to keep him detached from the pain as we progressed towards the summit. As we pulled up to the fighters who had already finished, we simultaneously fell to the floor, pumping our lungs with crisp oxygen. I looked at Sok managing to squeeze out just a few words, "From now on I'm calling you the Big Buddha Champion."

Again Sok tilted his head back towards the sky and laughed. "From now on, I'm calling you Turbo. Cause you're too bloody fast!" We laughed it off and limped our way to the bus that took us back to camp.

That night, Sok invited me for a victory dinner off of camp to celebrate our climb. "I know this great place that makes unbelievable fish. Truly something epic, it's about ten minutes from here. Jump on your motorbike and follow me." Without hesitation, I put on my helmet, hopped onto my rented red Vespa scooter and we began to ride. It was dark outside and I had no idea where we were going, but my instincts told me I could trust Sok's sense of direction. We passed the local market, the mall and started moving more towards the jungle.

After about fifteen minutes, Sok signaled me to pull up next to him. "We're almost there, mate. Just ten more minutes, stay on my tail."

Ten more minutes? I thought. *I'm sure everything is all right.* We continued to ride as we distanced ourselves further from the camp. I suddenly identified with Dorothy from The Wizard of Oz when she said, "I don't think we're in Kansas anymore." There were no buildings, no people and what once appeared to be dark, now looked like midday. At that point, I started hearing lyrics of the classic Guns N' Roses song 'Welcome to the Jungle'. "You know where you are? You're in the jungle baby!"

As the additional ten minutes expired, I pulled up next to Sok to get an update. "Sorry mate. Just got a bit lost, but I know where we are. Just a few more minutes."

How in the world is this the second time in this trip that I am lost in this jungle? I pondered. I had nothing to lose and decided to keep playing follow the leader. We continued to ride, as the roads became hills and the occasional street lights became non-existent. You could not see much on each side except for thick dark forests through which you could not even squeeze a needle. All I could really say to myself was a silent prayer of *God save me!*

After twenty more minutes of riding Sok came to a complete stop. I pulled up next to him, took off my helmet. "What's up? Where are we?" I asked.

After a moment of silence, he suddenly broke out into his Buddha like laughter. "I have no bloody idea brother."

Being influenced by his 'Ausi-ness' I responded, "Mate, how can you be laughing right now? We're lost in the middle of the freaking jungle!"

He shared his genuine smile. "Brother, the best way to get to know places, the best way to know yourself and the best stories in life, all start when you get lost."

I remained silently petrified. But as I looked back at Sok, I started to smile and also break out into laughter. Our cheers echoed through the jungle until our abdominals ached of pain. I did not have control of the situation anyway, so why not have a laugh? As we sat there on our scooters, in the middle of the jungle and in the middle of the night, my eye suddenly caught a familiar sight. "Hey Sok, isn't that the back side of Big Buddha?"

It had turned out we rode in circles for about forty-five minutes and were then lucky enough to get ourselves back to the local urban area. Sok now followed my lead as we made it back to civilization. We even found the local Thai restaurant Sok was talking about. We raised a toast to our wild adventure and immediately picked up on our philosophical conversation, filling our bellies with some freshly caught fish. Breakfast with Kings at its finest.

As we concluded yet another epic evening, Sok offered to cover the bill on account of the fact that he got us lost. He was not a particularly rich man, but he loved to surprise and spoil people all the time, just as a genuine act of love. As the waiter returned with his change, Sok looked over to a family seated several tables away. There were two adults, a teenager and a young child sharing a large bowl of noodles mixed with different meats and vegetables. He looked over at the waiter and said, "I'd like to cover their bill as well. Could you please bring me their check?"

I looked at Sok as the waiter left. I was unsure of his intention. "What are you doing man? Do you know them?"

As he paid the waiter for the family's dinner, he said in a boyishly excited voice, "No. Let's get out of here before they know it was us!"

"You don't know them!" I responded in complete disarray. "You don't even want them to know you paid? What kind of prank are you pulling?"

With his thick Aussie laugh, he responded, "The best one! Just imagine the look on their faces when they ask for the check. Let's go!"

Over the next month, Sok and I would share many more radical adventures, from training sessions to scuba diving excursions and crazy nights out on the town. Each experience provided me more opportunities to learn from his values, attitudes and beliefs. I deeply treasure his wisdom and friendship, and consider myself privileged to have gotten lost in the jungle with this philosophical King. Sawadee kap.

Extending Comfort Zones and Conquering Peaks

Throughout our lives, opportunities present themselves, but we do not always recognize them as such. We give them different titles like challenges, tribulations, failures and struggles. However, behind each of these masks lies the potential platform for growth and self-discovery.

I did not know much about this man, but when he was presented with the opportunity to do something that he had not done in years, which is beyond challenging (conquering the Big Buddha Run), he instinctively grinned and was immediately onboard. Reflecting upon this, I now think to myself, *How many opportunities do I grab hold of that really take me out of my comfort zone?* Many of us claim to be spontaneous, but in actuality, we seem to be so only in the realms of our life that we are familiar with. Hence our potential growth becomes strictly limited to what we already know. Therefore, when we extend our comfort zone of spontaneity, we part take in self-exploration on a whole other level.

Throughout our time together, Sok endlessly pushed his comfort zones, exemplifying the importance of inviting novel opportunities, especially the ones that may present failure. The climb towards personal growth begins here. The concept of climbing is perceived differently by everyone, but by observing the Big Buddha Champion's attitude, I learned that true climbers are not ones who effortlessly conquer peaks, rather they are the ones that battle their way to the top. They fight to discover their true limits and enjoy the exhilarating view (both simultaneously and at the apex). After a short celebration, they begin to look for the next challenging summit to ascend. This is the core attribute of personal excellence that leads us forwards in our pursuit to achieve our ultimate self, but it all begins by pushing ourselves in new realms in ways which we are unaccustomed too. So now ask yourself, what new mountain do you wish to conquer? What is your Big Buddha Run?

Above it all, the combination of the two forces of extending our spontaneous comfort zones and conquering peaks provides endless humble learning opportunities. As the famed Greek philosopher Socrates once said, "To know, is to know that you know nothing. That is the meaning of true knowledge." Discovering how little you know is simply a modest opportunity to discover what you can ultimately learn.

Royal Food for Thought

- Which comfort zone (that you normally do not challenge) would you like to extend?
- What peak (that you normally avoid) will you attempt to conquer?

Get Lost!

I sincerely believe that in life, you are always at the right place, at the right time, for the right reason. However, this philosophy became much harder to apply while finding myself lost in the Thai jungle with a stranger named Socrates. But it was exactly at this moment that I understood that the process of getting to know oneself must begin by first getting lost.

If you have gotten lost before, it means you were willing to explore new territories that were previously unknown. You were willing to expose yourself in a new way that caused you to reassess your character, leading to your discovery of new personal and untouched abilities. The establishment of your character becomes greater when you get lost as the only possible subsequent step (unless you give up), is to be found. Just as in Hollywood, any climax in life becomes more exhilarating when preceded by a treacherous valley because that is the opportunity for the protagonist to ascend.

If I were to ask you to recall the moment in which you experienced the most pride in your life, I guarantee that just prior to your moment of victory was what may have appeared as an immovable obstacle. You may have been physically, mentally or emotionally lost, yet despite the heavy layer of fog, you managed to get out. But not only did you get out, you did so with a new trait and sense of hardiness thereby founding a well-established feeling of personal pride.

Sok was the King of getting lost because rather than freaking out, he embraced his position with a genuine Buddha-like laughter. He knows that his position will only serve his knowledge of the territory, his character and future relationships. Thanks to our experience, when

I get lost, feel lost or am even just at a loss for words, I strive to tilt my head back and laugh while accepting that all conditions are perfect. Then I begin to find my way out of the jungle.

The next time you get lost, will you also laugh at the sky believing that conditions are ideal, or will you drown yourself in a pool of frustration and self-victimization, keeping you lost in the jungle of misery?

Royal Food for Thought

- When was the last time you got lost (physically, emotionally, spiritually)?
- What skill or value did you gain from doing so?

Humble Daily Random Acts of Kindness

Recognition. Most of us in this world seek various forms of recognition in the eyes of friends, family members and even people we do not know via different means. However, Sok introduced me to a new concept of acting out of kindness without the goal of external appreciation. He simply had the desire to surprise a fellow human being. This powerfully humble act, would not allow him to reap the fruit from the experience he created, rather he would simply have to believe in the positive power of the surprise he left for the fortunate family.

Many social and spiritual circles in life teach us the importance of daily random acts of kindness, but by doing so without the goal of recognition, we connect to a higher force. A stronger power in which we are focused on the actual good it creates for others and not solely the good it allows us to feel. This form of humble generosity is amongst the highest forms of giving we can perform. Attaining the belief that our actions are creating a better world that we may not see brings our game of contribution to a superior level. As is so wonderfully put by the character of Socrates in Dan Millman's book *Way of the Peaceful Warrior*, "There is no higher purpose than service to others."

I recommend you to openly invite the chance to perform such a contributing act. Keep your eyes open for the chance to provide good and just before you allow yourself to indulge in the spoils of the experience, walk away. Leave – believing that you have served as an influential co-creator of a beautiful occurrence for a distant human being. When you do, you will truly understand why we are referred to as 'man-kind'. That is what life is all about. We will not be able to see everything that we create and ultimately leave behind, so why not take the opportunity to practice such humble random acts of kindness?

The collection of these lessons and mindsets reveals the true mental strength required to be a fighter in the ring of life. Placing ourselves in front of new challenges, getting lost with laughter and acceptance, and acting to improve others' lives without recognition, is amongst the more powerful mindsets of a champion.

Royal Food for Thought

- Try performing a humble random act of kindness. Be creative. It can be a high five to a stranger, picking up someone's tab or any other deed that will serve others. Prior to receiving credit, flee the scene. How does this act of kindness compare to other acts you have previously performed?

3

THE CHERRY ON TOP

"The dream is free, the hustle however is sold separately."
-ANONYMOUS

Some names and identifying details have been changed in this chapter for security reasons.

We are each driven by a dream. It is equivalent to the golden cherry that sits atop of our mountain, and that you can only try to imagine indulging in it's exotic taste. As kids growing up, we are generally told, "Dream big! Shoot for the stars!" We are consistently asked, "What do you want to be when you grow up?" It is almost as if the taste of the cherry is an inseparable part of our character from a young age. While growing up, we never considered the possibility of not becoming that person. However, what we are not told is that in order to enjoy this prized fruit, you first must climb the hazardous mountain which always holds hidden obstacles.

My cherry was to become a fighter in the Israeli Defense Forces (IDF). I always loved Israel and wished to serve it as best as I could. I researched different units I could potentially serve in, from the navy to the army to the air force. I met with different fighters and officers from various units until I locked eyes with my final decision. I wanted to serve as a fighter in Israel's Combat Search and Rescue extraction unit. This elite combat unit combines the skills of a medic with a world-class fighter with the purpose of saving the lives of wounded soldiers and pilots that have fallen behind enemy lines. Their missions also include saving average citizens who are stuck in the worst of accidents. Whether it is on land, the desert, or the heart of the sea, this unit answers the call, fulfilling their slogan taken from the book of Psalms, "In times of trouble, you call and I will save you." In order to just be accepted to the training course, I would have to compete with four thousand applicants in a series of physical and mental examinations. The final of these tests is called a *gibush*.

A *gibush* is a physical assessment that extends over several days, with the goal of discovering which of the final applicants is physically, and more importantly, mentally tough enough to potentially become a prestigious fighter of the respected unit. We left home for one week to compete against the top two hundred applicants. The tests consisted of hours of crawling on thorns, days of sprinting and climbing sand dunes, long marches with stretchers (which at times exceeded two hundred and twenty pounds in weight), treading water for extended periods of time and little to no food and sleep. Only forty-six would pass the *gibush* and be accepted to the unit's training course (eighteen months). Of that group, only thirty will make the final cut to become distinguished fighters and future commanders of the unit. I'll let you do the math.

I wanted a position in the top thirty and I was ready to push my limits to get there. I trained four times a week climbing sand dunes, carrying weighted sand bags up hills, crawling through anything remotely thorny and even joined the local swim team to get the extra edge in the water. I was nothing short of a modern-day Rocky, working from the crack of dawn and willing to do whatever it took to be accepted into the Harvard of IDF units. I went for it all and wouldn't you know it, I made the cut!

The exhilaration of success was never so euphoric! I felt so gifted and grateful to discover such purpose at a young age. Although I did not really have anyone to celebrate with aside from my family (as I was still new to the country), my heart was content, knowing that joining this unit would bind me to a new potential band of brothers.

The morning of my draft, I felt like a golf ball in a blender. I shifted rapidly from anxiety to excitement, from fear to bravery, from anticipation to hesitancy. Just before I boarded the bus, I received a final tear-jerking kiss from my mother and a heartfelt hug from my father, as if they were releasing me into the wilderness to fend for myself. Despite the whirlwind of emotions, I felt ready. I had achieved 'success' as legendary coach John Wooden coined the term: "Success is peace of mind, which is a direct result of self-satisfaction in knowing you made the effort to do your best to become the best that you are capable of becoming." I had attained this peace of mind.

We were introduced to our new fellow comrades (of the forty-six who were drafted, we were split into two teams of twenty-three) and despite the excitement of meeting my new family, there was a bizarre tension in the air. We knew that only fifteen people from each team would make the final cut. This always reminded me of the hit reality television show 'Survivor'. The goal is to build the strongest tribe possible, yet to do so people must be eliminated. Such mental strain creates stress, agony and particular challenges for both reality television and real life.

With almost all the team members present, it was time to meet our new sole parent and guide, our commanding officer. We waited silently in the darkness of the stinging dry desert air until suddenly our sergeants ignited blinding red flares that burned close to our eyes. As the flares began to dim, an average height man with short blonde hair penetrated through the residual smoke. It felt as if we were being initiated into a prestigious fraternity, and we were standing in the presence of the grandmaster. He stood silently, staring at us for almost a whole minute, not saying a word nor expressing any emotion. "My name is X," he said in a cold voice (the actual name cannot be disclosed). "I'm your commanding officer." His body language gave away no emotion. None of us knew how to read him, but two things immediately became evident to us all. The first was that this training course would be the most arduous thing we would have ever done in our lives. The second was that our future in the unit would be solely determined by X.

With no time to waste, we immediately started taking both physical and mental beatings, while simultaneously studying our hopefully future profession. The physical aspect was nothing short of a nightmare as we were endlessly punished. When we failed to complete the impossible tasks set for us, we were punished by having to complete thirty burpees (from a standing position, fall into a push-up, jump to your feet, jump in the air while clapping above your head) in a minute and a half (feel free to try a set). If we did not succeed (which we never did), we would repeat the punishment, again and again and again. This sometimes extended for hours, occurring in the middle of the night, and even became the cause of injury for many of us, causing infected blisters, shin splints and even muscle tears.

The intensity of the physical challenges did not slow down, as we would surprisingly be woken up in the middle of the night to go on weighted marches through the mountains. The marches became longer (forty-five miles), the weights became heavier (at times drastically exceeding our own body weight), yet the drive to taste the cherry of success was prominent and still driving.

More challenging than the physical aspect was dealing with the constant heavy fog of the unknown. It felt as if I was standing at the bottom of a mountain covered by a thick cloud with only the view of the peak in sight. Never did we have any knowledge of what challenges awaited next. I recall one time we were driving back to base and were told to put on our Speedos to prepare for a two mile ocean swim. The bus suddenly stopped on the shoulder of the freeway as our sergeants barked, "You have seven minutes to prepare for an eighteen mile march. Go!" We always had to be on our toes, ready to pivot and immediately act, just as we would if we were to become official fighters of the unit.

Despite the detrimental effects this mentality had on my diet (losing and gaining large portions of weight in short amounts of time), my sleeping habits (occasionally going days without sleep), and creating a great deal of personal anxiety (I should have seen a psychologist), my mouth was still salivating as I so desperately wanted to taste the cherry at the pinnacle.

Yet the greatest battle was dealing with the mental humiliation. Usually, when we pass our mental borders, we are accompanied by a motivating figure who provides guidance. However, this was not the case, as we would be consistently reminded by our sergeants about our nothingness and why we should quit. Any means to create additional mental friction was added (a compulsory element of the training). On one occasion, I was even placed in front of the entire unit and scolded at for deciding to read a book while the members of my team were asleep on the bus. I was accused of being selfish and wrong for not trying to communicate with others.

But at least there was a relationship while being scolded at. With X, it was simply pure indifference, no positive or negative feedback. This pure lack of emotion generated boundless tension as we never knew what he was thinking. His apathy haunted us with an anxiety that lurked in the back of our minds twenty-four hours a day. The thoughts became voices asking, *Will I make the cut? What does he think about me?* Despite the extensive unease, all I could think about was how bad I really wanted that damn cherry!

After twelve tenaciously strenuous months of training, we were down to thirty-one. There have been cases in which a little over thirty have made the cut and therefore a deceiving optimistic view portrayed itself. Having come so far, I knew in my heart of hearts that I could not give anything more of myself, and I could live with that. It was at this point on a Saturday night that we were called in for a team meeting. X wished to discuss the training missions that awaited us that week, along with their potential hazards. The team always remained silent in these meetings as nobody ever wanted to risk becoming in disagreement with X. We all understood with whom the power truly laid. Between each of his sentences, all you could hear were the crickets outside chirping.

After almost two hours of silence, the meeting was about to be adjourned as X came to his final statement. "I have one final question before we finish. Who is the team idiot?" Never had we had been asked such an unconventional question like this before. All I could recall was looking at each one of my comrades thinking, *Idiot? All of these guys are unbelievable!* Again, crickets.

"I want an answer, who is the team idiot?" The room remained silent for another thirty seconds. All eyes remained locked on X. "I assume from the way things have been going that Doron is!"

In an instant, my world had suddenly crumpled. The man who held my dream in has hands, not only perceived me as the weakest link, but had now also projected to the whole team that I was the team idiot. At this progressed stage of training, this was an unexpected dagger to the heart.

I began telling myself, *Doron, don't react. Keep your cool, count to ten and then respond. One, two, three…*

"Can I say something?" A teammate raised his hand. I became excited as I prepared for reinforcements. "I agree. Doron really has shown he isn't the smartest guy during certain moments."

What did he just say? I yelled inside my own head. My face remained motionless as additional hands began to rise. Different members began to share their general consensus with X as I began to feel genuine betrayal. Each word pierced through me, unexpectedly stabbing me in the back as I heard the famous Julius Caesar quote "Et tu, Brute?"

echoing in the back of my head. I became washed over with shock and disappointment. This was the result created by the pressure-pot-like atmosphere of the unit; either you are with X or you are against him. I sat motionless listening to each syllable of every word said. When X asked me for a response, I nodded my head from left to right.

In almost an instant, I shifted from a state in which I finally had found a band of brothers in a new country, to one of standing alone and having been mentally shot down. I had to make a decision. Should I walk away with my self respect over all that I had achieved until that point thereby forfeiting my continuation in the course, or battle the circumstances as an outcast attempting to climb this Everest in a whole new fashion? I shared the experience with my parents at home. "They don't deserve you. Go to a different unit and hold your head up high." My inner logic agreed with them, but all I could think about was that goddamn golden cherry that had so long awaited me at the top.

I decided to stay, but for the time being, I was going to set some new personal standards for myself. These boys were no longer my brothers. Family supports each other, not tears one another apart. X was no longer my father figure. A father does not humiliate, he provides values and teaches how to become a good human being. I would go all in and leave the ball in God's court. The consequences of this decision translated into social isolation in every sense of the words.

That following week was amongst the most intense weeks of my life. With a grand total of six hours sleep and almost no food, we completed a weighted march of over thirty-seven miles, navigated through an additional twenty-four miles of forest, and crawled through razor-sharp thorns that cut through our uniforms and even into the meat of our skin. But above all else was the challenge of doing so alone. My sole focus was the cherry on the top. I no longer cared about the humiliation, I did not care if I had to fight an army companionless nor did I care about any of X's opinions. I was going to attain my goal.

As the week concluded, I stood at my watch post for my shift with barely any feeling of my legs beneath me. Suddenly, I was approached by X for a personal conversation (these rarely occurred). "Your performance this week was outstanding." He said in his monotone voice. "You exceeded all of your abilities drastically. Keep this up, and you will surely finish the training and join our unit as a fighter."

Despite all the internal animosity I held toward him, the power of hearing that was beyond elating and was equivalent to being told that I had just hit the jackpot! Without revealing any signs of vulnerability, I celebrated inside my mind while looking him dead in the eye and coldly responded, "Okay." Over the next month and a half, I regained my confidence and continued to deliver results. I successfully patched up some of the relationships with the team members as I understood that they too were placed in a difficult position. I now felt as though I had come out of this dark valley smarter, stronger and with a new appreciation of what family is.

One Friday afternoon, as we were to be released for a short weekend leave, we were sent home with navigation homework. We would have to study for a twenty mile solo navigation in the Negev desert, so that we would be able to immediately complete this mission once we returned to base. I studied the whole weekend to make sure I would be on my game. I wanted to achieve my highest score yet. Upon returning to the base, we were each required to complete an oral exam, proving our knowledge of the territory we would be navigating to one of the inspecting officers. I approached one of the officers and answered his questions flawlessly. I received high marks, being told, "You are going to do great." I was walking tall. My gear was inspected by X, again being told, "You're good to go! Get on the bus." I placed my equipment on the truck, grabbed my M4 rifle and sat on the bus with the rest of my team. As the engine rumbled, my mind and heart were at ease. I was ready.

I closed my eyes for the long drive to the desert until I suddenly heard one of the sergeant's voices. "Everybody onboard? Good. Doron, get off." I grabbed my gun and jumped off to see X standing outside. The bus began to drive away and I suddenly feared that my cherry was going with it. "Grab your stuff from the truck, put on your dress uniform and meet me at the Major's office." As soon as he finished his sentence, I knew my time in the course had come to an end. I was about to be ceremoniously removed from the unit.

I showered quickly, put on my dress uniform, shined my shoes to a polished charcoal black and walked over to the prestigiously ranked officer's building. Different fighters who had already completed the training wished me good luck and farewell as I passed by them. They also shared with me that the decision to let me go had already taken place several days earlier prior to our weekend release. This only intensified the sting of the humiliation.

I deeply inhaled, said a silent prayer and firmly knocked on the door. "Come in," said a deep voice behind the door. I walked in and saluted the unit's reigning officer. As he saluted back, my eyes temporarily shifted to X who was seated next to him with his usual cold stare, just slightly softer. The Major began to speak. "Doron, over the last thirteen months, you have excelled as a soldier in our strenuous training regimen. Your fellow comrades speak highly of you (this was very surprising), and you are appreciated by your commanders for pushing yourself harder than most (this was extremely surprising). But at this moment, we feel you do not fit what we are looking for. You are being released from the unit."

My cherry disintegrated in an ambiguous mist as the reasons provided made no sense to why I was being cut. Yet through the clutter of emotions of confusion, anger, and pain, I found a single legitimate sensation that appeared to make sense. Acceptance. I knew that despite all that had been done to me both physically and mentally, the unit was unsuccessful in making me utter the words "I quit," and I could accept that I delivered my very best.

"Is there anything you would like to say?" The officer asked as he and X curiously affixed their gaze upon me.

Despite feeling that I was looking at the broken pieces of my shattered dream spread throughout the Major's office, I immediately returned to reassess what drove me towards my prized cherry. What was my true cherry, my true dream? I reflected for a moment until it suddenly became clear.

I straightened up my head and looked at the decorated officer straight in his eyes. "I thank you and the unit for the opportunity to serve here. But with all due respect, sir, my goal was not to serve in your unit. My goal was and still is to serve this country to the best of my ability." Both the officer and X appeared to be dumbfounded by my response. I was content with my understanding, which took me more than thirteen painful months to internalize.

I left the unit that night, and did not hear back from X or my teammates. They were now down to thirty and I was left to find a new way to attain my well deserved cherry.

How Bad Do You Want it?

In recent years, social media has been flooded with endless motivational content, and in one way or another, they all seem to propose the same question. "How bad do you want to succeed?" As inspiring as they are, many people seem to show great difficulty in truthfully answering this, because their desire is not up to par with their actions. They claim they want to be rich, healthy and in a loving relationship, but when the time comes to get your butt on the field, there is little to no hustle. You can pray for the rain, but be ready to deal with the mud. You must be willing to work! In order for me to succeed in my service, I really should have asked this question while acknowledging the mud. When I am alone, humiliated and my hands uncontrollably shake because of reasons I am not aware of, then how far will I go to get that cherry?

If your goal is to run a marathon, find your soul mate or to succeed in your discipline and you are not there, take a good hard look in the mirror. Ask yourself, "On a scale of one to ten, how badly do I want to achieve this?" If your answer is ten, you are going to find a way. If your answer is anything less, you are going to find an excuse. Please understand that a score of "ten" is reflective of your effort, not your outcome. This answer means you will continuously do everything in your power to pursue your goal and grow. You will work hard enough that the surrounding circumstances will no longer be able to provide a threat, because you just keep returning even more robust, thereby never uttering the words, "I quit!" If you stick to that you will find your way, and believe me, there is always a way.

The encompassing circumstances created by X, the sergeants and the unit, allowed me to truly get a glimpse of what I can do when I want something bad enough. These series of events happened as they did and despite the pain and humiliation I endured, I remained driven to succeed and got closer to a ten than ever before. As long as your desire matches your hard work, you are going to find a way to enjoy your cherry.

Royal Food for Thought

- What do you wish to succeed in? What is your personal cherry?
- From one (the least) to ten (the most), how badly do you want to succeed?
- If your score is less than ten, what do you need in order to increase your effort and get to work?

Why Do You Want It?

Many of us know what we want. We want to be rich, powerful, healthy and happy (not necessarily in that order). However, that desire is not enough to reach it. In order to create a 'way' you must firmly establish a 'why'. Why do you want to achieve this goal? The 'why' is the root of all actions and is always present, but many of us just do not take the time to acknowledge it. This process requires deep thought, sincere reflection and transparent introspection. But I will tell you that once you know your 'why', you become an unstoppable force that holds all the cheat codes to the game of life. You develop a sense of character that relentlessly returns stronger with every setback you face. It is a beautiful thing.

With that said, I believe that X understood that emotional indifference towards another is much more challenging than any kind of relationship. I would like to believe that his position through each of our confrontations was motivated by genuinely wanting us to more deeply explore our personal 'why'. The deeper we had to go, the more disconnected he appeared, causing the resilient ones amongst us to discover the root motivation of why we chose to serve in this unit. Whether this was his intention or not is irrelevant. By my focusing on the taste of the cherry, I thought about what I wanted (to serve in the unit), but it was only after I was released that I understood why I wanted it (to serve my country). If I was more connected to my 'why' during this time, I believe the outcome would have differed.

Challenge yourself to explore your 'why'. Go to the foundation of your drive to truly understand - why are you doing this? Will it serve just you? What ideal is inseparable from your character and will help you passionately find your way? Go down this rabbit hole and you will find that as your 'why' becomes greater, your 'way' becomes easier.

> **Royal Food for Thought**
>
> - Look what you are most passionate about in your life and ask yourself, "Why am I doing it?"
> - Once you have analyzed your 'why', how can you utilize it to serve others to solidify your role as a Queen or King?

A Kick in the Butt…

This was amongst the greatest challenges I ever faced. Dealing with the immense physical pain, exasperated emotional anxiety and unrelenting loneliness, was no fun adventure. Even more so, many of us take such experiences from our lives with a silent belief that we could have done without them and that they were meaningless. We look at them almost as if their presence is directed towards our destruction. Yet, despite several subsequent years of pain, anguish, and anger towards X and his tactics as an officer, I truly am grateful and humbled by his ways and by what he provided me (intentionally or unintentionally). He brilliantly orchestrated an opportunity to fully embrace and explore the values listed in this chapter and those that follow. My perception of this reflects that I decided to allow the circumstances to serve me, rather than my serving them.

When serving the circumstances, we take what has happened and firmly grab onto it, finding power in our pain whilst inflating our ego like a hot-air balloon. When expressed, it is usually paraphrased in various sentences such as, "You don't understand, what he told me…" or "Despite everything I've done, she…" In such a state, we continuously empower the situation and unknowingly turn ourselves into victims. The common denominator between these sentences and mindsets is that we are only considering our position while pointing our finger. We put the blame for our misery on the world, thereby becoming powerless and enslaved to what has happened. The final result is that we become the victim of our story and are ultimately confined by the circumstance.

But have you ever noticed that when you point one finger at somebody else, you are actually pointing three fingers back at yourself? Meaning, when we blame another, we should be willing to take three times the responsibility and search for what we can claim responsibility for. In such a manner, circumstances come to serve us, as we take what has happened and find power, value and meaning through it.

But in order for all of this to happen, you must accept the following message. If you choose to take just one value from this book, I hope you choose this one. **We control nothing in this world!** We have no control over our future, we have no control over our success, and we even have no control over whether we will make it to our next appointment in fifteen minutes. At any given moment, an anvil can crash down on us from the sky or a terribly devastating accident can occur (God forbid) and turn your world upside down. You have no control in this world over anything! **Except for one thing**… and if you shift your attention and pinpoint your efforts to this, you will never become a casualty to life's circumstances again. That is, **how you decide to deal with things mentally.** It is a shame to waste our time empowering what has happened and is not in our control, when rather, we should shift the energy into a way in which we can harness it to strengthen our character. Why should we trouble our minds with something over which we have no influence? Even the fundamental principle of physics in the law of conservation of energy declares, "Energy can neither be created nor destroyed; rather, it transforms from one form to another." Shift your mental energy and transform what has occurred to you, into a triumph!

Beyond all the challenges I experienced in the unit, the team meeting with X was emotionally traumatic for me. Yet thanks to that meeting, I discovered values that helped me write this very book and work with thousands of people worldwide. Regardless of his intention, I learned that each event, person and circumstance can be benefited from, to discover a greater internal power or unknown dormant resource. This is how we get stronger, develop as human beings and endlessly connect with royalty.

To sum it all up, just remember. A kick in the butt brings you one step forward. The question is, are you focusing on the pain in your butt, or that you have moved one step forward?

Royal Food for Thought

- Return to your most challenging experience. Are you still serving it, or is it now serving you?
- How has this event served you in your life today?
- How has it served others? What are you going to do, to make it help more people?

4

A LION AT
A TEA PARTY

"Extremes are easy, strive for balance."
-COLIN WRIGHT

Following my release from the unit, I was invited to a series of interviews for different units that offered to pick me up off the free agency list. I would ultimately be reassigned to serve in a Special Forces infantry unit that specialized in demolitions and combat engineering. Beyond the challenge of acquiring this new profession's knowledge and skills, my true test of character was in my ability to join a new line of brothers who had trained together for approximately a year. It was almost as if I was adopted by a foster family, except that they were not looking to adopt. Naturally, I worried about how I would be accepted amongst them. Would I be an outcast again? I knew I could not succumb to the fear which would keep me in place. It was time to get back in the game.

I showed up bright and early to my new base, located in the heart of the Israeli desert, the Negev. The heat was scorching as my dress uniform became decorated with impressive arm pit sweat stains. I waited outside to be called on by my new officer. I baked in the sun for several hours, slowly turning to a darker shade of my skin tone until I finally saw my new authoritative figure. He was a tall, skinny man with short dark hair that kind of reminded me of a stick figure. He definitely did not seem tough enough for his rank. Even from a distant, he seemed relatively soft and kind, which was radically different from X.

He invited me to sit, and we began to discuss my background during my time in the former unit. He shared with me his high hopes that my unique skill set would propel my new team forward. I was not sure if I was the answer he was looking for. All I could do was to reply, "I'll do my best."

He became overjoyed to acquire a new ally and began to share with me the status of the team. Nothing could prepare me for what he would say next. "The team is broken. They are not well disciplined. They have great skills, unbelievable strength and unique abilities, but the motivation just isn't there. We need a soldier to positively influence and drive this team in the right direction." His eyes then gawked at me as if I may be the messiah he has been desperately praying for that could bring water to his part of the desert.

I paused, not really knowing how to respond as I still had not met anyone from the team yet. The awkward silence intensified and all I could think to myself was that I did not want to let him down on my first day. I gulped. "I'll do my best."

We shook hands, and he directed me towards my new team's crooked tent. "Go to sleep. You'll be woken up in the morning." Again I felt like a golf ball in a blender feeling a mixture of anxiety, excitement and confusion. I lay alone in the massive tent, closed my eyes and told myself, *Wake up in the morning, and take it step by step. You'll get it done.*" I slowly dozed off into a deep sleep. Later that night, the team would enter the tent from a practice mission they had, not having even noticed I was inside.

"Doron… Doron… Wake up!" I opened my eyes and saw the blurred image of my new officer's head poking through the curtain of the tent. "I want everybody up in two minutes and in full gear. Go!" I sprung out of bed as though I was shot out of a cannon! I began to dress in full uniform while screaming to my sleeping comrades, "A minute forty-five, let's go!" I was moving fast and wanted to show the officer that I was the soldier who could be that change. "A minute fifteen boys! Move, move, move!" I began to prepare my equipment for inspection. "Thirty-seconds, everybody out!" I checked myself one more time to make sure I was set. "Time!" As, I raised my head, I became haunted to discover that nobody was there. No officer, no teammates and I stood alone in full gear, ready for what felt like a one-man war. I remained motionless as to not get in trouble. *Did I just dream that? What's going on?* Three more stagnant minutes passed until finally the other team members began to slowly exit the handicapped tent. Some were underdressed, wearing nothing but their boxers and a pair of crocs, while others decided to just stay in bed. I now started to understand what the commanding officer meant by 'broken'.

The team was the recipient of more than enough punishments by alternating officers and sergeants. Ironically, to my somewhat inconsistent delight, the penalizing system in the unit was based much more on the physical than the mental. Time and time again, our team would be punished for not completing tasks or for not working fast enough. In all honesty, it was not that the team lacked the ability to do so, they were just lacking basic motivation. The officers used these sanctions as a form of revenge for the team's lack of an attempt to perform at their best level. This was a true shame, considering that the company was composed of some truly remarkable individuals with both untouched and underutilized potential.

Film writers could not create such colorful characters, as the unique attributes of each member exceeded that of the next. There were big guys, small guys, different ethnicities, different backgrounds and more variety than a build-it-yourself salad bar. But amongst this heterogeneous bunch, the one character that really seemed to stand out was Aviv. Standing well over six feet tall with the bodily features of a professional body builder, it was almost impossible to miss him. Every muscle was perfectly carved as if he was an ancient Roman sculpture. The only feature that was disproportionate to his body was his small egg-shaped head, which balanced between his towering shoulders. In every physical task we would perform, he would get psyched up by ferociously roaring as if he was a lion intimidating its prey in the African safari. Every time he would release his inner beast, we would be frightened, feeling as if we were the ones being hunted down.

Despite possessing the anaerobic physical strength to lift a tractor, his energy levels depleted quite quickly, as he would progressively grow lethargic. This led him to almost always having something in his mouth to snack on. At any given moment when speaking with him, he would always be chewing on something to restock his energy levels. Yet beyond his trademark physique, snacking habits, and animal-like instincts, he possessed a heart of gold. He was the kind of guy who would always come to a teammate's assistance, regardless of the status of their relationship. Everybody knew that there was something special to him.

One night, we were "routinely" punished for showing pure disregard for our weekly equipment inspection. By now we had become accustomed to these physical penalties which generally included crawling on stones and thorns, countless inclined sprints and the all-time classic, everlasting push-ups. This time however, one of our creative sergeants decided to enhance the sanction by combining all the above while having us wear gas masks, thereby limiting our oxygen intake. Now in addition to the physical stress, we could barely breathe as this continued for several painstaking hours. Our muscles continuously grew heavier until we were finally released around two in the morning.

We entered our tent drenched in sweat and soaked in mud as we tried to remove the infinite thorns from our limbs. Each member understandably began to curse the sergeant. I must admit, there was a great deal of creativity with the strong foul language used and even I joined in expressing my dismay. Everybody was shooting off verbal shots, except Aviv. After several minutes of hollering, I noticed his silence. "Hey man," I turned to him. "You were with us this whole time, and you have nothing to say about this bastard?"

Aviv paused for about ten seconds and began to contemplate deeply. The whole team redirected their focus towards him in curiosity of what he would say in his deep beast-like voice. "Listen, the guy is just really…." He paused. "Really…." We leaned in closer in great anticipation. "Mean."

"That's it?" A fellow comrade shouted. "After all that, that's all you have to say?" The rest of the team dismissed his response as invalid until it suddenly hit me. He was not responding from emotion as the rest of us were. He took the extra time to analyze and accurately choose the word that best expressed his position. He perfectly paired his emotion with its descriptive vocabulary term, making his reaction all the more powerful. None of us saw it coming.

As the months passed and our training progressed, I started connecting more with the team, finding my place in this new family. The physical tasks increased in difficulty as we approached our final exams. There were three final exams that would require us to combine all of our abilities that we had acquired since the day we were drafted. First, we would have to perform the "Northern Exam." In teams of two, we would have to navigate approximately sixty-two miles, from the Sea of Galilee to the Mediterranean Sea, in four days.

The territory was built of steep mountains, treacherous valleys and dense forests through which you could not see. Each member would carry a backpack weighing roughly sixty percent of their body weight, consisting of an outdated communication device that looked like several metal phone books stacked on one another, six liter and a half bottles of water, several cans of tuna, and additional rocks for those who were punished. Our task was to stealthily progress at night without being caught by patrolling officers in the vicinity. During the day, we were to find a hiding spot to camouflage within the scenery.

Teams were predetermined by the officers and I was fortunate to be paired with a trusted comrade, Farkash. He was a good navigator and we were both in excellent shape, so I was pumped. We began with climbing a mountain at a forty-degree angle out of the Sea of Galilee. A single misplaced step and we could have tumbled hundreds of feet down into a dark abyss, but together we conquered the peak and moved onwards to the first checkpoint concluding the first night.

As we rested in our disguised bush, we received a message through our communications device that Farkash was being released from the exam to attend to personal matters. He was called to leave our hiding spot and get to the nearest patrol vehicle to transport him. As Farkash took his equipment and walked away, I was not sure how my navigation would progress being on my own.

I lingered with my thoughts until I suddenly heard footsteps coming through the bushes. I turned my head in fear that an officer had found me and was gratefully surprised to see Aviv. "Aviv, what are you doing here?"

While approaching me, he responded in his bass line voice, "My partner was also removed from the navigation. We've been reassigned." I was unsure if this was good or bad, but I did not really have much of a say either way. We exchanged high fives and wished each other luck.

The second night commenced as we started the navigation again with a brutal climb to the peak. "All right Aviv, let's push it. We'll get over this hill then slow down." We were on pace as Aviv ferociously growled his way like a predator through the bushes. However, his speed steadily declined with each step. It was the type of deceleration where I noticed every couple of minutes that I was a dozen feet ahead of him and was forced to wait in place. It felt almost as if I was repetitively watching a slow motion highlight reel of Aviv marching on. As we increased in altitude, Aviv decreased in stamina. After an hour and a half of pacing, we reached the summit, excited to discover an easy plateau ahead. "Let's keep moving." I anxiously said. But it seemed that Aviv was becoming more lethargic as his growls converted into drowsy huffs and puffs. He was a big guy, carrying a lot of weight, and we were not advancing at the speed we needed to.

The brush of the forest became thicker in the barely lit night and I grew restless just wanting to reach the next checkpoint. I could not handle this game of 'catch up' any longer. Daybreak was upon us and I knew that something had to be done. "Aviv, grab on to my bag." I told him bitterly. "Hold tight." As soon as he grabbed on I began to jet, pulling the combined weight of Aviv, myself and our equipment. I pulled him for dear life, ceaselessly repeating to myself the mantra, "A little more… just a little more…"

The night finally concluded and we arrived to our checkpoint before dawn. My legs were immensely grateful for the several hours of rest. Unfortunately for them however, the second and third night would not show any compassion, as he became even more burdensome. That translated into more weight to pull, accompanied by his obnoxious roars. As his body sank in the opposing direction that I pulled, my thoughts began to sink accordingly. *How the hell did I get 'so lucky' to drag the big heavy guy through the mountains?* My blood began to boil as my antagonistic rage fueled my mental engine, which dragged the both of us. Now I was roaring and grunting, pulling Aviv, showing no signs of sympathy.

By the final night, I was mentally shattered and had to talk to myself just to get through the exam. *Doron, I know this sucks but just one more night. After this, you and Aviv won't have to do this again.* I hauled, pushed and fed my internal motor with animosity until I fell apart at the finish line with Aviv on my rear. The exam had come to a close and I physically felt like a building being demolished by a propelling wrecking ball.

Thankfully, we were given one week to recover and prepare for our next test, the 'Southern Exam'. A fifty mile, four-night navigation from the general area of Be'er Sheba to Masada with conditions that were similar to the Northern Exam. The key difference, now we would be navigating through the desert. Night time would be pins-and-needles freezing (motivating us to keep moving to stay warm) and the day would be scorching hot (forcing us to minimize movement). However, none of that faded me as much as hearing the officers call our pairs. Wouldn't you know it, Aviv and I were together again. *Just my luck!* I thought. Although I was physically recharged, my mental muscles were still disabled. I was not ready to do this again, but just as before I did not really have a choice.

The navigation began and it seemed that the only thing that changed was the landscape. Aviv again was holding on to my bag as I was sprinting for dear life with my anger fueling my energy. *This is unbelievable!* I screamed inside of my head. *How could this happen to me again?* My thoughts lingered heavily over those next four nights only adding to the surplus weight I was already heaving. The only consoling thought I had was imagining punching Aviv in the face and watching stars circle his head like in the old cartoons. In retrospect, I deeply regret not redirecting my focus to the stars shining above our heads in the desert sky. I am sure they were amazing.

By the time we reached the finish line, I became entirely indifferent towards him. I was relieved knowing that the final exam was a 'Team Exam' and no longer would I be solely responsible for carrying the drowsy beast. In all honesty, I did not want anything to do with him at that stage, which was a harsh thing to say considering he was a fellow comrade. I felt as if we were two brothers at war.

The 'Team Exam' required the whole team to complete a weighted navigation of approximately sixty-two miles while intermittently performing various practice missions, testing our ability to synchronize our newly collected skills. We understood the difficulty of this enormous challenge. However the prize at the journey's end kept us driven. We will finally have become official fighters and completed our training. This is amongst the highest honors bestowed during one's military service, and we all wanted a taste of that glory. We prepared our equipment, studied our maps and were ready to commence.

The first night spanned an eternity as our commanding officer was unsuccessful at navigating, ultimately getting us lost and adding another six miles to our total distance. Each additional step became crucial as the total distance we were to reach was close to our physical capacity. In all honesty though, as long as I was not carrying Aviv, I could have marched another twenty miles.

The second night only got worse as the team was punished for talking during the march. We were rewarded with carrying two dummy mines, weighing thirty pounds each. I was the lucky one to receive one of them and add it to my load. My equipment was now closing in on a total of one hundred and twenty pounds. My legs gave in with every momentary stop, with my body tumbling into the ground. But still, as long as I did not have Aviv on my back, I was mentally sound.

During the third night, I fatigued, suffering from a psychological heat wave. I had to cross the finish line in order to become a fighter in the unit, but my mind could not envision it. My feet were swollen with blisters, my muscles were tensely cramped and there was almost no blood circulating to my arms, as my backpack's straps were pulling the carried weight in the opposing direction. My head pounded like the drum line from the Disney film *George of the Jungle* and my mental game officially shut down. I pathetically dragged my feet to complete the night while silently mumbling to myself, "At least I don't have to carry Aviv."

With the final night came a tsunami of adrenaline. I was suddenly prepared for my movie-like comeback to finish strong. With eighteen miles to go, I kept my focus on the finish line as we marched hard. I began to loop a new mantra in my mind. *You're getting closer. Ignore the pain. Keep moving!* However, the toll my body had taken over the last month was far beyond its limits, and every step become more physically devastating than the previous. Despite my strong will and desire, already after the three miles, I could hear my body urgently reporting distress signals. *Mayday! Mayday! We're going down!* My speed rapidly decreased until I found myself in a physical stalemate. My legs came to a complete halt, gravity sucked me towards the ground and a flickering image of the final destination began to vanish. After everything I had gone through, from the struggles in my first unit, up until this very moment, my final night. It appeared as though I was not going to make the cut...

"I got you. Come on buddy, get up." I magically began to float to my feet as I felt two hands grab me from my backpack allowing for blood flow to return to my arms. "We're going to finish this. I'm with you." I turned my head and while in complete disarray, I saw Aviv. He held me up, told me to grab on to his bag and began to pull. "Hold tight!" Aviv marched and roared us through the next fifteen miles, carrying me in a somewhat poetic fashion. In between his intermittent lion-like roars, he would consistently cheer me on to keep my spirits high throughout all the missions that awaited in our final night. We would cross the finish line together to become official comrades of our unit.

I was genuinely humbled by the experience and embraced Aviv with a brotherly hug of gratitude. To this very day, Aviv and I remain close friends who joyously watch over each other, constantly share memories of our service and roar our way through obstacles. This was my first of many adventures with the King of the jungle.

Listen, Think, Speak

In our day to day lives, we are pressured to be up-to-date and to constantly contribute our two cents to an ongoing conversation. However, this can have detrimental effects on our communicative processes. I mean, how many times have you found yourself in a deep conversation with a friend who is sharing a problem, and while they are speaking, what you truly are listening to is your own voice in the back of your head, saying something like, "When he's done talking, I'll respond with this…" We are all guilty of this act. Rather than sincerely being present and processing the content of what we are being told, all we are preparing is what our response will be. This begs the question; are we really listening and providing the best answer?

As social creatures, we are expected to provide some kind of contributive and noteworthy feedback to ongoing conversations. However, since we are heavily influenced by the frantic, frenzy lifestyles of the modern age and are submerged in different worlds of instant media messaging such as Facebook, Instagram and Twitter, we feel compelled to provide instant responses. This misguided influence creates an illusion that the time to fully digest the presented information does not exist. We are left producing answers that arise from emotion rather than heartfelt thought, and this can have dangerous consequences.

When responding out of emotion, we do not take the time to fully digest the data that we have received. We access the directly available information in our mind and often times find ourselves saying things we never intended to say as we are misled by various cognitive heuristics. Beyond hurting our own reputation as a legitimate and reliable source, we provide false or lacking information for others to rely on, which can ultimately have severe consequences.

Although we were punished dozens of times, the memory of Aviv calling our sergeant "mean" remains extremely vivid. My fellow comrades and I were hurt and therefore instinctively turned to our emotion rather than fully analyze the situation and choose our words. Aviv chose a wiser route. He first paused, silently reflected and then articulated the exact word that expressed his emotional standpoint. He expressed heartfelt thought by defining his exact position in a proportional manner rather than using profanity to ineffectively slander another's name. Heartfelt thought requires five more seconds of processing, to really analyze the value of your potential contribution. In all honesty, despite never having heard some of the flagrant language used by my other teammates, we all agreed that Aviv's words were most accurate. Choosing our words as Aviv did leads us towards becoming empathic, mindful and accurate, and ultimately to offer our greatest personal input to the person with whom we are talking.

I challenge you to be fully present in your next conversation. It is much harder than it seems. First, process all of the data entering your mental hard drive. Then, mindfully analyze all the knowledge you have been given. Stay as committed to the present as possible. Do not draw on information from your immediate memory or from unreliable sources. Sincerely attempt to allocate any resourceful contributions you can provide while delivering your essence. Then and only then, speak. The goal of the game is not to provide the fastest answer, but rather the most meaningful one. Listen, think, speak.

Royal Food for Thought

- In your next conversation, whether it is with a friend, partner or in a group, use the "Listen, Think, Speak" method. Was your contribution to the conversation more meaningful than usual?

Put down Your Mental Luggage by the River

There is a wonderfully powerful Zen parable that tells of an older and younger monk, who together came to cross a river. They approached the river cautiously as they observed its strong current. At the crossing, a gorgeous young woman stood somewhat petrified. She turned to the monks and asked, "Can one of you please help me get across the river? I cannot swim."

The two monks froze in place, as they looked at one another knowing they had each vowed to never touch a woman.

Suddenly, in a single swift movement, the elder monk placed the woman on his back and began to swim for shore. The younger monk gazed upon the two and remained speechless as he watched the older monk taking action. After crossing successfully, the elder monk placed the woman down and continued to walk with the younger monk for the next hour, without exchanging a single word.

After an hour, the younger monk could no longer contain himself and exploded unexpectedly. "What were you thinking? As monks, we cannot touch women! We vowed to never do so and you have held this commitment for decades! How could you dare carry her?"

The elder monk gently smiled and replied, "Brother. I set her down on the other side of the river. Why are you still carrying her?"

During the Northern and Southern exams, I was unsuccessful in letting go of my painful mental luggage on account of my immature mental status, which was thoroughly experiencing anger and pain. I found legitimacy in my emotion and therefore let it dictate my thoughts and behaviors. Often times, people add extra mental weight in order to justify a feeling they are experiencing, only to later learn that the only person they are hurting is themselves. I have no doubt that had I decided to put down this excessive baggage, I would be both mentally and physically lighter. The experience will always be the experience; the question is, how do we decide to take it?

We all find power in our pain. This power comes in different forms. When we are hurt, people come to our assistance. When we are sick, people begin to call and visit us. When something is wrong, people come to our side. But if this form of power is played out too long, it ultimately becomes detrimental, damaging both our own physical and mental well-being. This is us trying to strengthen our position, through weakness. Therefore, I invite you to take the opportunity to find a different route by first putting down your mental luggage down by the river.

Royal Food for Thought

- Can you recall an experience in which you leveraged your power through pain? What were the consequences of doing so?
- Had you put your mental luggage down by the river, would have you performed differently? If so, how?

The Tea Drinking Lion

A dear mentor of mine, once told me, "Be like a lion at a tea party." What he meant was, on one hand, be a fighter. Be a tough son of a gun who does not take crap from anybody and fights to achieve all of his goals. Yet simultaneously, know how to be a kind and polite soul who knows how to be respectful of others. Respect all, but fear none. Knowing how to successfully balance these two forces is essential to all success. Think of a star basketball athlete sprinting down the court, bulldozing his way through the competition towards the hoop. With such forceful power and momentum, in order to be able to score a lay up, the player must be able to release the ball gently off of his fingertips and softly graze the backboard. Knowing how to balance any two opposing forces in life is the attribute of true masters.

In my opinion, the ability to give help and the willingness to receive help are amongst the hardest forces to balance in life. Surprisingly, for many, the latter can be more challenging, as they feel giving does not endanger their ego. However, what I did not understand was that Aviv was not trying to take advantage of my assistance, rather he simply took the help he needed. His King-like attributes became more evidently apparent when he pounced on the opportunity to deliver help and balance the scale. Not in the sense of helping me because I helped him, but rather because he is an all-natural tea-drinking lion, exquisitely balancing between the extremes of life.

Furthermore, Aviv managed to exemplify this equilibrium while lifting me to the end of the Team Exam. On one hand, he demonstrated great physical strength and aggression in order to drag me to the end, yet at the same time, he was authentically sincere and encouraging, helping me maintain a strong morale.

Despite having known the quote my mentor told me years ago, it was only at this moment that I fully appreciated its meaning.

Royal Food for Thought

- What two opposing forces must you balance to achieve success?
- Is it easier for you to give or receive?
- Are you able to ask for help as much as you give it?

5

A BEAUTIFUL MOURNING

"Growing up your generation has everything but really has nothing. Growing up we had nothing, but truly had everything."
-CELINE MAMAN

I cannot genuinely say that I grew up with a rough childhood. I was born and raised on the sunny shores of San Diego, California. The United States' capital of beaches. My childhood was not like some of the remarkable stories of celebrities and athletes who grew up without parents in the roughest streets without a dime to their name. Sure we had tricky moments that we maneuvered through as a family, but I know I was blessed with two lovingly supportive parents and two gifted siblings who despite many obstacles provided me far beyond three meals a day and a place to lay my head.

However, my parents grew up under very different circumstances. My father grew up dirt poor and would tell me stories of how he explored piles of clothing donated by various charity groups. He was born in Morocco and moved to Israel at the age of four after his parents divorced. Together with my grandmother (his mother), they moved to a small fishing town in the north of Israel called Akko, where my grandmother remarried a Hungarian fisherman who was a resident of the city. My father spent his time as a boy roaming the streets with friends, working in a local factory, lying on the beach, and playing as much soccer as possible. That was all they had and according to him, that was all he needed.

My grandmother was a busy bee. Until she remarried she was the only source of income for her family and therefore did not have much time to raise her children. The only viable option was to have them raised by her parents (my great-grandparents), Moshe and Ladisya. My great-grandfather, Moshe, was a heavy smoker with something of a gangster-like mindset. According to my father's stories, when the town hall asked him to pay his bills, he would show up unannounced to the mayor's office and release a bag full of snakes on his desk. He would only remove them once he was granted a pass on the expenses. At the same time, he was a caring and passionate family man who end-lessly showered others with hugs and kisses. My great-grandmother, Ladisya, was a domestic housewife who always put the family first: answering everyone's needs before her own, constantly stepping up to the plate, providing anything she could for all members of her family.

The unique combination of these two characters resulted in a household upheld by the oldest of old-school values (probably more so thanks to my great-grandmother). My father and his younger siblings had these values imprinted upon their brains, which included hard work, respect for elders and forbidding the use of profanity. Naturally, this greatly impacted my father's stature.

My mother was raised in a very different environment. She and her siblings were raised in a strict household in the roughest of neighbor-hoods. The kind of neighborhood where either bad things happened or bad news was delivered. During both the Six-Day War and the Yom

Kippur War, dozens of families in her vicinity were notified of loved ones who were killed in battle. The fragile buildings did not protect her family very well from the cold, only making the circumstances a bit more reflective of her reality.

She was the third of four children. Her father was a baker and her mother was an accountant, and were both highly respected during their time in Morocco. But upon moving to Israel, they had to do their best to adjust and adapt to the circumstances in order to provide for their family. Matters did not get any better as my mother's brother (the eldest of the siblings) and father were surprisingly drafted in 1973 to fight in the Yom Kippur War (one of Israel's most devastating battles). My uncle was badly wounded and lost almost all of his fellow comrades in front of his very eyes due to a tank explosion. He made it out alive, but this obviously made things very difficult. My mother and her remaining siblings remained in an underground bunker with my grandmother, only to continually hear alarming attack sirens occurring aboveground. To this very day, she is still reminded of those times when sirens are sounded.

Yet, through it all, my mother was a fighter at heart who found release in the form of dance. She was (and still is) a passionate dancer who bounces around the dance floor like an Energizer bunny in a pinball machine. She loves rock 'n' roll, folk dancing, and even the occasional swing dancing. She was so talented that she was even invited to take part in a short European tour in her late teens to perform for various Jewish communities. The immediate gratification granted through her moves has kept her feet moving until this very day, where she is always the life of the party. Even at weddings, the DJs generally find themselves calling it a night before she vacates the dance floor.

Although my parents grew up in the same tiny country, they each were exposed to radically different worlds. The beauty of their relationship was that despite their different backgrounds, they were raised on a similar premise. This notion is reflected in a mantra I have heard my mother repeat for years. "Growing up, your generation has everything but really has nothing. Growing up, we had nothing, but truly had everything." This powerful understanding has been imprinted upon my brain, developing some form of positive, internal, silent jealousy of the life lessons they acquired through their childhood experiences and struggles. Fortunately, this jealousy drove my desire to learn some of those same values they attained. They greatly serve me today, and hopefully will continue to do so in my future.

One day, during eighth grade, I returned home from school. This was that time of life when puberty retaliated with acne, my weak position on the social status pyramid was my prime concern and basically I was not a mature, active citizen of the world. I was only functional within my own microcosm. As I entered my home, I was surprised to see my father, as I could almost never recall seeing him home before nightfall. Generally, he was always working until nine or ten in the evening. I asked him what was up and what he was doing home so early. He responded with sorrow, "Your great-grandmother, Ladisya, just passed away at the age of ninety-three. They are burying her in Israel in a couple days. I'm flying tomorrow morning."

I could not believe it. This was the first time I knew somebody personally who passed away. She was the sweetest lady, who always seemed to be celebrating. I remember when we received an invitation for her ninetieth birthday. She invited hundreds of guests to this extravagant, Godfather-like event, all of whom were distant cousins of some form. The comedy, however, was that in the following two years, we received the exact same invitations to attend her ninetieth birthday party again and again. The events were just as joyous and she only appeared to grow younger.

This humble woman was not educated per se, nor was she the protagonist of an exceptional success story; she was simply a family woman made of love and happiness, never wasting any time on pain or anguish. During her final years, she fought a great battle with cancer and on more than one occasion was told by doctors, "We believe you only have a few days left, please prepare accordingly." She would sit in her hospital bed, laughing in their face that she would soon be out. As soon as the doctors' allotted time expired, she would leave the hospital with her head held high and roll into the closest casino to play the slot machines she loved. This was the spirited Queen who raised my father and had now departed from this world.

I attempted to embrace my father but understandably received a relatively dry response. I headed to my room to reflect on both her life and her death. I knew that her siblings, children and grandchildren would attend the funeral when it suddenly hit me. I understood that her succession rate in this world was represented through the fourth generation; my cousins, my siblings and myself. *Who would represent us?* I questioned. I felt that the final 'layer' had to be present at the burial in order to bring her life and death to a full circle. I approached my father again and shared my thoughts. "Can I come with you? I want to represent the fourth generation." My father grinned, talked it over with my mother and granted my request after short deliberation.

The following day, my father and I boarded our flight to Israel via New York. During the combined sixteen hours of flights to Tel Aviv, I became filled with mixed emotions of excitement and anxiousness. Despite being raised in an Israeli household, I had only been in Israel once at the age of five. My only family there was my mother's distant relatives (whom I never met) and my biological grandfather Eli (my father's father) who I had only met twice. Furthermore, Israel was not in its most peaceful time as a wave of terrorism was in full effect, with premeditated attacks and suicide bombers exploding in different major locations in the country, taking innocent victims with them. Combine all of that with the fact that I was going for the purpose of attending my great-grandmother's funeral, and I had plenty of food for thought on this exhausting trip.

As soon as we touched ground, my father and I disembarked the plane, hopped into a taxi and headed towards my great uncle's house in a small town named Azur, just outside of Tel Aviv. We were only staying there for one night, as the funeral would already be held the following morning. After the service, we would then stay in a hotel in Tel Aviv.

The jet lag was devastating as the ten-hour difference made both my father and I feel like sleepwalking zombies. As soon as we arrived to the house, my head plummeted into the pillow and I fell into a deep sleep.

"Doron, time to get up." My father woke me and I did not even recall falling asleep. "The funeral is in an hour." I grabbed my luggage with my toothbrush in my hand and headed for the taxi parked outside. The cemetery was located on the eastern side of Jerusalem on Mount Olive, considered to be Jerusalem's holiest mountain as it is believed that this is where the messiah will land when he comes down from the sky. Being buried here generally meant you were either someone very special who had great influence or you invested in this permanent real estate much before you departed.

We pulled up to the top of the holy mountain, where my family members congregated. Everyone was in attendance as I stood as the youngest member amongst the group. They all stood outside a modest single-floored cement building with their heads hung low in despair. I embraced each of them with a hug, not really knowing what to say or which facial expression to portray. My head was filled with jargon and I was deeply confused.

I was still waking up from my sleep and was now trying to confront this completely novel situation. I needed to freshen up. I pulled in my father and whispered in his ear, "Can I go to the restroom before the funeral begins?" He placed his hand on mine and nodded his head. I innocently entered the building and began to walk the hall searching for the restrooms. I passed the first two rooms, finding nothing but locked doors. Door number three, however, was open. I confidently entered, expecting to have found what I was looking for. I stepped in and instantaneously became petrified as I found myself standing in front of the lifeless corpse of my great-grandmother. Every muscle in my body tensely contracted, every thought in my mind became immobilized, and I stood for a solid minute in a pure state of shock and horror with that image presented before me. I was alone in a room with a deceased family member. Every one of my neurons fired forceful action potentials signaling "Run!" But my eyes stayed affixed on the corpse and my feet remained glued to the ground.

Suddenly, I heard a deep manly voice from behind. "What are you doing here, kid?" Without attempting to recognize the individual I sprinted for dear life as if I was competing with Usain Bolt in the one hundred meter finals of the Olympics. I dashed through the hall way, carved the turns in the building and blazed past all of the ceremony's attendants straight into my father's arms. I broke out into tears. Once my father understood what I saw, he stayed by my side for the remainder of the funeral. The state of shock prevailed within me as my mind raced at a million thoughts a minute as my father tried to calm me down. "I know that was a hard sight to see, but the ceremony is almost over. From here, we'll go straight to visit your grandfather, who lives nearby. We'll disconnect a little." I nodded and remained silent as I kept my head fixed on the ground.

I was hesitant making contact with my family after the burial as I was still in a state of awe. We got a cab and drove to my grandfather's house. I tried to suppress the thoughts of the funeral and redirect them towards the curiosity of seeing my grandfather. I had only met him twice during my life, and all I could recall was that he was an introverted man with a bad limp. I knew that he and my father were not always on the best of terms as he did not play the most active role in his life. But anything to get away from what I had just experienced seemed nothing short of a dream.

Personally, I was surprised that my father wanted to visit him. I asked myself, *Would I want to visit a man who was virtually nonexistent in my life?* This notion was only further intensified when I understood that my grandfather had asked my father and one of his brothers to send him monthly payments of five hundred dollars as their business in America was thriving. This continued for over fifteen years, even during his times of major financial debt. Honestly, I was disgusted.

The taxi pulled up to an old torn down building. We opened the cab door and were slapped by a rancid and contaminated smell. An aroma of sewage combined with rotten garbage that should have been taken out months ago. We began heading for the building and ascended the stairs, cautiously approaching my grandfather's apartment on the third floor. With each step we climbed, the ferocity of the smell only became viler. This was undoubtedly the worst fragrance I had ever inhaled in my life.

We stood at the door of the apartment as my father knocked while covering his nose. The door swung open as if we were in a haunted house. Old static opera music was playing in the tiny one and a half room apartment. "Dad?" My father called out. As we passed the almost non-existent kitchen, we saw a pan on the stove with a piece of meat that had already turned green from the amount of time it had been there. Simultaneously, the refrigerator was serving host to an array of foods that were far beyond their expiry date. We turned the corner to find my grandfather lying in his bed, blankly staring at the ceiling. His thick beard indicated that he had not shaved in months. He laid motionless under a series of heavy blankets next to his ancient radio. He smelled as if he had not showered in weeks, and looked as if he had not had human contact in years. I immediately stood corrected as this became the new most challenging image I had ever seen, easily surpassing that of my great-grandmother's corpse.

The stench began to burn our eyes as my father tended to his father, cleaning him up. This was not the image either of us expected to see. My father, being the kind of man he was, began to tell him, "I'm coming back in a few days. I will not allow my father to live like this." Later in the trip, my father would hold true to his promise, thoroughly cleaning the apartment and replacing all the blankets and towels. He even hired a person to come twice a week to cook him a decent meal and properly tend to his needs. The five hundred dollars monthly payment, however, would still continue regularly.

We entered the taxi again to leave the apartment. I had no words left to express the day's events. There were no thoughts left to console me. I began psychologically self diagnosing myself, convinced that having seen all this at such a young age, I would be scarred for life. Beyond my own personal trauma, I could not even imagine what my father was going through. First burying the woman who raised him, then seeing his fathers' gruesome living conditions. The driver ignited the engine, as my father turned towards me in the backseat. "Doron, take off your seatbelt and lie down. I'll wake you up when we stop." I did not even want to know where we were going next. Without any hesitation, I laid across the back bench and dozed off into a slumber.

"Doron, wake up. We're here. Take off your shoes and let's go."

My shoes? What was he talking about? I sat up straight and squinted my eyes to find that we had arrived to the Gordon beach in Tel Aviv. There was a strong salty scent that was accompanied by a beautiful blue sky and crystal-clear water awaiting by the shore. I was sure I was dreaming. "Where are we?" I asked.

With no explanation, he grinned and responded, "We came to play some beach soccer. Let's go!"

"Beach soccer?" I asked. "I just saw the two most traumatic images of my life and you want to go play beach soccer?"

"Come on, let's go already!" I took off my shoes and socks, and followed my father. We did not have bathing suits, so we simply stripped down to our underwear and began to play with another six men who were playing on the shore. I was never a good soccer player. In fact, I was actually quite bad, but I did not really care about that then. All I could see was that I was together with my father on one of the most beautiful beach shores on the Mediterranean, surrounded by authentically happy people who were joyously chasing after a round piece of bouncing rubber, all while laughing hysterically. I absorbed the rays of the sun while having the time of my life. Despite my generally poor level of skill, my father still claims that it was the best soccer I had ever played. We played for about two hours until the sun retreated into the horizon. We sat together on the shore, talking only about the game. It was the most beautiful day of my adolescent life.

What Do You Really Have?

To the naked eye, it appears obvious that the conditions in which my parents were raised were far from ideal. If you think about it, the conditions in which most people from a low socioeconomic status are nurtured appear far from optimal. However, it is only when people take the time to recognize what true treasures they possess that they will always find something both powerful and contributing. For example, one can develop abundant creativity from a lack of materials. From a lack of technology, one can develop excellent communication skills. From a lack of parenting, one can sustain a brilliant drive to become a fantastic mother or father figure. However, this is all a choice.

The fact is that circumstances cannot be changed. Whatever has happened has happened, and we have no control over that. So deal with it! The only thing we can control is our decision of how to mentally navigate our developing character. One can either become further damaged and emotionally impaired or take advantage of the opportunity to transform this obstacle into a stepping stone of growth, excellence and personal values.

This reminds me of a fascinating parable about a bitter and cruel father who was an alcoholic and drug addict, who had almost killed himself several times. He served a twenty-year sentence in prison for the murder of a liquor store cashier. He had twin boys, one of whom grew up to be just like him. A drug addict and thief who was put in jail for attempted murder. His brother, however, raised three beautiful children, enjoyed his marriage and was sincerely content in his life. He worked as a manager for a major national foundation and kept physically fit while refraining from both alcohol and drugs.

How could these two young men have turned out so differently having been raised in virtually the same environment? Both were asked this question privately, unaware of the other's response. Surprisingly, they both provided identical answers. "What else could have I become, having been raised by a father like that?"

Find the precious value in whatever it is that you have or don't have, and become that excellent person. Strive to be like my mother; if you are growing up with nothing, find the way to make it your everything.

Royal Food for Thought

- What condition must you accept to pivot your state of mind towards meaning and value?
- Look at all of your possessions. What is it that you hold which truly defines you?

Do the Right Thing in Every Context

Doing the right thing in our world has gone through a peculiar evolution over the last several centuries. It appears that historically, we started out with the concepts of right vs. wrong, good vs. evil and other similar contradicting motives. However, over time, this began to change within the context it was found. In other words, it appears more so that doing the right thing is only the right thing when the circumstances are right. Think about it. We all agree that it is crucial to keep our world clean and save the environment, but many of us refuse to pick up trash that we did not litter. We all believe it is important to assist the elderly, but only do so when they are our own relatives. The examples are endless, and yet all exemplify the same notion: that our understanding of wrong and right in this world is all dependent on the context in which it is done.

I will not lie. I was somewhat surprised by my father's willingness to help my grandfather, let alone initiate a visit. This was a man who took almost no part in raising him, remaining invisible for most of his life and was entirely detached from his world. However, the values that he learned from not having an active father drove him to recognize that this was a man in need who could not perform almost any hygienic or sanitary function to properly care for himself. In my father's eyes, all previous history between them became irrelevant and the current context shifted into the spotlight. Now all that awaited was the chance to do the right thing and care for another human being.

A year after my grandfather's death, we learned his true story. He was a kind and simple man who refused to spend any money on himself — he saved all of the money my father and uncle sent. He kept this money in the bank, accumulating just over one hundred thousand dollars (with collected interest), which he saved for us. As he was so truly humble, he did not seek any form of recognition. It was the final twist in this epic plot. Unfortunately, it was only after his death that he was revealed as a King that I wish I got to know better.

The context is always changing and with the addition of new information, our perception of the situation can drastically alter from one extreme to another. There is always more that lies beneath the surface, and it is for that reason that the concept of doing the right thing should stand independent of context at all times! Keep this understanding in mind as you progress through your own journey, as your time to step up to the plate and do the right thing will also come.

Royal Food for Thought

- What small action can you take in order to do the right thing?
- Have you ever discovered a piece of information only after you have acted that has completely altered your perception? How did this new data change your position?

Flip the Script to Accept

The more that day progressed, the more I wanted to reach its end, knowing I would never have to relive it. However, as the day concluded, all I wanted was for a few more hours of sunlight to continue playing to solidify this truly timeless memory. My father has always had the ability to instantly flip the script of life. To suddenly make a sharp yet perfectly calculated turn in order to change an experience for the better. That day, which began with death and ailment, ended with a powerful sunset and the fullest experience of life.

The true brilliance of this characteristic is beyond the ability to choose the story setting or prominent characters in the scene, but rather mastering the sole factor that is completely in his control, his attitude. He had no way of controlling or changing the events that occurred. These events were equally if not more traumatizing for him than they were for me, yet he made the conscious decision to do something radically different. I do not mean playing beach soccer, but rather to shift his mindset towards an empowering question, "When else will I have the opportunity to spend time with my son playing soccer on this amazing shore?"

Viktor Frankl stressed this notion in his world-renowned book *Man's Search for Meaning (1946)*. In his book, Frankl shares his tragic, inhumane experiences, surviving the Holocaust and how it led him to finding meaning in his life. His story would lead to his development of logo-therapy; a therapeutic technique founded on the belief that human nature is driven by the search for a life of purpose. One of the underlying factors to discover this purpose lies in relinquishing the feeling of control. It is about appreciating that we do not have control over our life's events. As he concludes his book, he shares how he reflects on his experience on the massacre of the Holocaust. "Everything can be taken from a man but one thing, the last of the human freedoms, to choose one's attitude to a given set of circumstances, to choose one's way." Such a mindset allows one to perfectly master the ability to benefit from challenges and always to keep your head in the game of life.

Our point of focus directs the script of our life movie. We will always find power and legitimacy in whatever notion we decide to focus on, whether it is pain, joy or any emotion in between. We will rationalize, identify and apply countless defense mechanisms in order to accept our position. But to live a life of greatness, we must make it our responsibility, to choose our mindset wisely. This choice is always in our control and thus gives us an unlimited ability to flip our script at all times, just as this righteous King did.

Royal Food for Thought

- Think of a moment in which you were mentally or emotionally stuck. What could have you done to pivot out of that state of mind?

- Accepting that all is perfect is amongst our greatest challenges. What can you do in order to become more accepting of the circumstances you have been gifted?

6

FALLING OFF THE DESKTOP

"One doesn't discover new lands without consenting to lose sight,
for a very long time, of the shore."
-ANDRÉ GIDE

There are some truly mind-blowing places to travel in this world. Usually, our eyes feast upon computer desktop images with stunning scenery as we wish were there rather than our 'boring' day to day lives. The accompanying feeling while gawking at these jaw-dropping sights is that they are light-years away. That their sole purpose is to be a backdrop on our screens to restore an illusory feeling that there is something beyond our world of work. People do not generally envision themselves dipping their toes in the waters of these photos; rather they place it in sight, so there is something 'nice' to look at. I guess we just sometimes get so caught up in working to make money, that we never really take the time to enjoy spending it. This reminds me of the Dalai Lama's brilliant answer regarding what most surprised him about humanity. "Man. Because he sacrifices his health to make money. Then he sacrifices money to recuperate his health."

As I faced these stunning images on a daily basis, I questioned what was my motivation to work? What was it that I really wanted? Understandably, money was a logical motivator. Everybody wants to be wealthy. But so many people spend their lives working hard to make money that they never seem to really get to enjoy. I have heard it so many times before; we make money doing things we do not enjoy, to buy things we do not need, to impress people we do not even like. Elders would tell me that at the end of our lives, we eventually each make our imminent return to our initial starting point only to rediscover and re-appreciate the gifts that we always had. They referred to the simple joys like the feeling of a heartfelt hug of a child, hearing the laughter of a loved one or smelling the mesmerizing aroma coming from the kitchen when the family is preparing a festive meal.

But as I became further absolved into the engulfing matrix, I developed an appetite for more. I grew hungry to explore the world and discover its secrets. I meticulously inspected different images thinking, *What if there was such a place? What if these two-dimensional depictions could become the setting of real life adventures?* I was eager for something new and was already mentally set to 'explorer' mode. I decided that I was going to travel in a computer desktop.

I endlessly researched different global destinations, until I serendipitously discovered the ultimate haven. New Zealand. A hidden Garden of Eden off the Tasman Sea, which remained as God's hidden masterpiece. Idyllic beaches, breathtaking mountains, crystal clear lakes and the vibe of a transcendent serenity which appeared to be nothing short of paradise. The country, being nearly double the size of the state of New York, hosts less than five million people and nearly thirty-million sheep. This nirvana is perfectly harmonized by a single one of their cities, Queenstown; the world capital of extreme sports. This city had anything you could imagine, from cliff repelling to whitewater rafting, bungee jumping to canyoning. The collective awaited adventure would serve as my ultimate escape.

I worked for four years, saving every nickel I could, and was accepted for a unique advocacy program that would get me all the way to Sydney, Australia (just a three-hour flight away). I would finish my work just prior to the Jewish high holidays, giving me ten weeks to bring this colored desktop to life. As the months rolled by, I completed my research, set my plan, performed my duty as an emissary and at long last prepared for my departure.

I set out to begin and conclude my adventure in Queenstown. I would journey full circle throughout the country to return to the city's most thrilling attraction, the Canyon Swing. From a record three hundred and fifty-seven feet high, this is the world's highest cliff jump. It begins with a free fall of two hundred feet, which takes your carried momentum into a pendulum swing of six hundred and fifty feet over the most stunning glacier blue river. With such a thrilling adventure waiting at the finish line, I could not wait to begin my trip.

Upon landing, I met another Israeli traveler by the name of Green. He was a short and sturdy fellow who shared many similar philosophies such as mine, yet above all else, we were both looking forward to taste the flavors of life in a very novel way. We decided to join forces and continued our travels together.

We journeyed through challenging nature hikes, snowy weather and remarkable scenery until we decided to head up for the capital, Wellington. Green had reached out several weeks prior to a local named Roger, who served as a host for wandering travelers such as ourselves. Apparently, Roger had been doing this for over thirty years, which had me thinking, *Why would anybody be so willing to accommodate strangers?* However, the thought was short-lived, as I referred to his home as a pit stop until we would embark on our next adventure in Auckland.

We pulled up to a large white wooden house that stood on the outskirts of the city. I gleamed through the window only to see the inside pitch-dark. Green knocked twice on the large wooden door as we awaited a response.

The locks turned as the door slowly creaked open. "Can I help you gentlemen?" An old man with thick glasses and thinning white hair under an old golfer's hat stood behind the half-open entrance. Despite his injured right arm, which was tied in a sling around his neck, he radiated the softest smile I had ever seen.

"Yes, we're looking for Roger." Green replied.

He embraced us as he stepped out of the doorway to pull us in for a warm one-armed hug with his brittle limb. "I'm Roger." He said excitedly with his thick Kiwi accent. "Welcome! Come. Come inside."

We were not expecting to be received so warmly as he brought us in with an open arm. As he turned on the lights of his home, we discovered wall-to-wall murals of ancient Christian references. We were not sure if we had arrived in Wellington or the Vatican. There was no question we were in the home of a deeply religious man.

He escorted us through his grand tour, pointing and reading out various Biblical citations that were painted on the walls. "This is one of my favorites," he would say excitedly. "Do not let kindness and truth leave you; Bind them around your neck..." He would then move on to the next one. "And I absolutely love this one. 'Do not neglect to show hospitality to strangers, for by this some have entertained angels without knowing it.'" I could now see his motivation beaming through him.

He eagerly jumped from verse to verse as if he was a curious child exploring a fascinating museum for the first time. After ten minutes, he finally began to calm down as he normalized his breathing and tranquilly exhaled. He had served us an extravagant buffet of religious wisdom, only to leave us with one more message before he let us be. "You know boys, I can go on for days. But in the end, what we must all strive for is beautifully summarized by my favorite passage. 'Love thy neighbor as thyself'. Store this understanding in your heart and it will be delivered through your actions." The sincerity in which he emulated and embodied this value through his incomparable hospitality was inspiring. As he wished us a wonderful rest of the day, I knew that at one point, I would wish to share a royal meal with this one-armed religious King.

The following morning, Green and I awoke hungry for adventure. We had to be back by nightfall, as that night was the beginning of the high Jewish holiday of Sukkot, one of the three harvest gathering festivals. It is customary to celebrate by building and living within a temporary dwelling known as a *Sukkah*. Generally it is decorated on the inside with pictures and hanging fruit. Green and I had no intention of building one as we barely had our own fixed dwelling. But daylight was burning and we wanted to make the most of our time.

I proposed that we explore the beautiful wildlife park of Zealandia, which was only several miles away. Green concurred on the condition that we ride there on mountain bikes through a challenging trail that climbed around the park along a hazardous cliff. I initially gulped, as I was not what you would call an 'experienced rider'. The only bike I ever owned got stolen after two weeks, and that was fourteen years earlier! I went back to my lesson from Sok: 'be spontaneous outside of my comfort zone'. "Let's get riding!" I declared.

We rented a pair of mountain bikes from around the corner and strapped on our helmets. Green showed off his professional off-road biking skills, utilizing every minor bump to perform an impressive trick. After thirty-seconds, I was convinced he was born on a bike. I, on the other hand, firmly grasped the handlebars for dear life, causing them to flagrantly wobble as I attempted to balance both the bike and my fear of falling. For the most part, I rolled the bike by my side and sprinted up the hill to catch up.

After about an hour, we finally reached the summit to enjoy a moment's fresh air and the breathtaking sight. I inhaled deeply to savor the quality of the crisp oxygen while Green seemed to be preparing for takeoff. "Until we get to Zealandia, I'm going to pick up the pace and stop occasionally for you to catch up. I just want to get my adrenaline pumping. See you soon!" Before I could utter a sound, he was off, curving down the dangerous pathway atop the ridge like a seasoned veteran.

I stood alone upon the peak looking down at the snake-shaped trail ahead in horror. Either way, the only direction was down. I decided to psyche myself up rather than psyche myself out. "You've got this Doron!" I exhaled slowly. "You've got this!"

I pedaled slowly as my focus remained locked on the perilous slope. My hands were now fused to the handle bars as I progressed cautiously. "Come on Doron!" I said out loud. "Focus!" I yelled. I slowly replaced my fear of falling with the belief that I was going to beat this mountain. And so I did. Suddenly, I was cutting side to side and picking up speed like an adrenaline junkie. My hands began to loosen as I screamed, "Yes! You've got it!" I was flying!

Then, in the midst of my over-inflated confidence, a gust of wind shifted my weight to the right edge of the pathway. The trail could not hold and caved in, taking me down into the cliff with a minor avalanche of rubble. My front wheel got entangled in an exposed tree root, launching me into two non-acrobatic aerial summersaults, as I rapidly rolled my way towards my possible demise. My body was tossed like a thrown rag doll, until my right leg slammed into a tree bringing me to a halt.

I screamed in agony. "Help! Help me!" My cries, however, fell upon deaf ears as I was completely alone. I was highly anxious but knew I had to calm myself down. "You're okay, Doron. Breathe. Let's do an assessment." It was time to play Dr. Maman. I examined my physical status from head to toe, thankful to find no protruding or broken bones. Despite my gratitude, I discovered a bloody mess around my right leg. It was stuck deep in an exposed branch of the tree that broke my fall. I yelled in torment as I aggressively yanked my leg out of the branch, only allowing for more blood to gush out. I was in need of immediate medical attention.

I crawled through the thorns and rubble back up to the trail. The hospital was not coming towards me, so I knew I had to get moving. I jerked my bike out of the tangled mess and started riding. With each pedal, I could feel more blood departing from my body. After several minutes, Green turned around and discovered my injury, joining me in my search for medical help. He proposed that we go straight to Zealandia rather than a hospital. He was sure they had a medical staff present, at least he hoped.

We continued to move as I grew woozy and lightheaded. I could feel my hands starting to slip as I grasped my bike firmly. My right sock and shoe were doused in warm blood, and my body was starting to feel cold. We pedaled hard for well over forty minutes, causing me to exercise more force on the pedal and thereby losing more blood from my penetrated limb. An intense tingling sensation ran through my right leg, feeling as if it were being charged by an army of ants. With every minute that passed my anxiety heightened, until we rolled up to the parking lot of Zealandia.

I gingerly hobbled off my bike and shifted all of my weight on to Green as he assisted me to get into the park's facilities. The building was surrounded by a tall encompassing gate, similar to that of the exhibit in the classic Spielberg film *Jurassic Park*. The automated doors opened as we entered. We were immediately approached by the concerned manager.

"Do you guys have any medical staff here?" Green asked with urgency. By then, I was calm, believing that I would finally receive proper medical attention.

"No, we don't." I instantly became pale as he flushed my last bits of faith out of me. "But we have a first-aid kit." I laughed out loud, knowing very well I would need stitches at best.

Green began to clean up my blood stains and scratches with various burning disinfectants that hurt almost as much as the fall. The manager was kind enough to organize one of their vans to transfer me to the nearest hospital, where I would receive several stitches and unfortunately have a sizable piece of meat removed from my leg that they could not salvage. It would take several months for the flesh to fully recover.

I taxied back solo to Roger's house with a mummified leg and a devastated soul. After having traveled for only ten days, I knew my trip would have to come to an end in order for my open wound to heal. I took out my phone to swipe through all the 'desktop' photographs I dreamed of seeing, knowing I would return home somewhat empty-handed. I had traveled to the hidden corner of the earth, only to be stuck in bed.

Then, a gentle breeze of gratitude came over me as I suddenly understood what I had been told by my elders about the essence of returning to that which I always had. After four years of work, twenty-seven hours of flights and one calamitous fall, I reflected and recognized on my true treasures which I always had: my loving parents, my loyal friends, my patient girl. I suddenly wanted to cherish each of these relationships exponentially, searching for every chance to say 'thank you' and utilize every opportunity to deliver a 'you're welcome'. Rather than be in dismay that my adventure would end sooner than expected, I slowly became filled with acceptance and appreciation knowing I had such true wealth to be thankful for. I immediately called my travel agent to reschedule my flight for the beginning of the next week.

I paid the cab and limped into the house leaning on the walls as to not exert too much pressure on my leg. As I shut the door behind me, I saw the back entrance to the garden was wide open. "Hello?" I called through the vacant religious halls. "Roger?"

His warm voice called from beyond the door. "I'm out here."

I sluggishly dragged my leg and remaining hopes for any 'desktop' adventures behind me as I exited towards the garden. Suddenly, I was blown away as I discovered a beautiful *Sukkah* in the back corner of the garden. "What do you think?" Roger asked with his authentically compassionate smile. He had built us our own temporary dwelling in his backyard, with only one arm. It had beautifully fresh fruit hanging from within that he had just picked. "I just wanted you lads to properly enjoy your holiday."

I was speechless. "How did you… I completely forgot it was… this is amazing!" I sighed as I could barely finish my sentence. I simply thought to myself, *Why would a man who's not even Jewish and is restricted in movement with one arm go so far to help us observe this holiday?* So I asked.

Not to my surprise, he responded with a grin, "What? You don't remember our conversation from yesterday? Love thy neighbor as thyself."

What a legend! I thought to myself. I was so deeply moved by his kindness that I asked him to sit with me, so I could share an officially royal conversation with this King.

As we sat, he noticed my bandaged up leg. "What happened?" He asked in shock as he could see the blood stains penetrating through the freshly wrapped bandages. As I shared with him my semi-heartbreaking adventure, he expressed the purest form of empathy. "Oh dear," he said with a sigh. "So what do you plan to do now?"

"I already have a ticket back home for next Monday. I guess I'll just rest," I said with a half, unauthentic smile.

He leaned forward on his chair to close some distance. "You know son, I'm sure you've noticed, but we have quite a lot of sheep in this country. We're outnumbered!" We both chuckled. "But honestly, they get me thinking a lot about life. You look at them and just see low-altitude clouds with heads. They'll eat grass, roam the hills and that's it. If we don't choose how to live our lives at every given moment, then there's little to no difference between them and us. Elders in my state wouldn't dare to think of doing the things I do, and let alone attempt to build a *Sukkah.* But I only wish to love you as I love myself, so therefore I do it." My eyes began to soften as I understood what he meant. "The way I see it, you have two days now to rest and five days to become more than a sheep. You can go find your adventure or be a sheep."

Over the next two days, I stayed in bed, sharing tea and great conversations with this wise and humble King about life experiences and their hidden meanings. Beyond his priceless gifts of spiritual value, he inspired me that being short a limb did not mean I could not explore. I left Roger's place with an open wound and a strengthened soul. I went on to go open sea kayaking (with a trash bag tied over my leg), glacier hiking (with two trekking poles to share the weight of my injured leg) and even jumped from the famed Canyon Swing in Queenstown. Between us, it was truly out of this world.

The Businessman and the Fisherman

A wealthy American tourist was at the pier of a small coastal Mexican village when a row boat with just one fisherman docked the shore.

Inside were several large yellow fin tuna fish. The tourist was amazed with the quality of his fish and asked how long it took to catch them.

"Not long, only a couple of hours," the humble fisherman replied.

"Why didn't you stay out longer to catch more?" asked the tourist.

The fisherman humbly responded, "This is more than enough for me to support my family."

"But what do you do with the rest of your time?" the tourist asked.

"I play with my kids, enjoy a siesta with my wife and take the evenings to stroll into the village to sip some wine and play guitar with my amigos."

The tourist recognized the potential at hand. "I am an investment banker, let me help you! Spend more time fishing to have a higher income and buy a bigger boat. With that income, you could buy several boats, until you eventually have a fleet of ocean liners! Then you could sell directly to the processor and open your own company. You could ultimately run the industry. You could move to Mexico City, and maybe one day to New York. There you could run your global tuna fish empire!"

The Mexican fisherman inquired about his vision. "But, how long will this all take?"

The tourist replied, "Fifteen to twenty years."

"But what do I do after that?" the simple fisherman questioned.

The tourist grinned. "When the time is right, you will sell your company and become very rich and make millions of dollars!"

"Millions? Wow! Then what?" asked the fisherman.

The American slowed down his breathing to respond. "Then you retire. Move to a small fishing village off the coast where you can play with your kids, take siestas with your wife, occasionally stroll into the village where you could sip some wine and play your guitar with your amigos."

I believe the takeaway from this parable speaks for itself. We spend our lives working so hard to make money and pursue our dreams, all the while chasing our own tails to the point of exhaustion, just to appreciate and rediscover what we had all along. Values, family, friends and all the irreplaceable joys in between. Do not wait for the finish line or an unfortunate accident to enjoy these priceless commodities. Before venturing off into the world, cherish and recognize the gifts you already have first. Then explore the world while remaining grateful for both your collected treasures and the ones you plan on accumulating.

Royal Food for Thought

- What treasures do you hold in your life that you overlook? What is it that you have always had that you took for granted?

- What can you do to remain grateful for that which you have while exploring for new valuables to add to your collection?

Love Thy Neighbor as Thyself

In the world of religion, this ancient commandment is found in the Old Testament, the New Testament, the Quran, and is discussed philosophically amongst virtually all beliefs. It poses possibly the most impossible challenge of them all. Most religious leaders place their focus on the first part, "Love thy neighbor." Being able to openly love and express kindness and warmth to all, regardless of background or beliefs. Most of us have enough trouble just trying to accept people who align themselves with certain political parties, let alone express affection.

However, the true greatness and essence of this commandment resides in the second part, "Thyself," meaning, "Yourself." It is about knowing how to love another as if they were you. You have to ask, how in the world is it possible to devote yourself to a stranger with the same intensity with which you are committed to yourself? How is it possible to care for another person, who holds the role of an anonymous character, in the same manner which you would be concerned for yourself? It is impossible! However, setting such a standard provides us with a master-level mindset for which to endlessly strive.

Roger humbly held this attitude, sharing this love with all. For more than thirty years, he brought in all wandering travelers, regardless of background, as if we were each one of his own kin. He dedicated himself to providing home felt hospitality along with sincere value, despite any obstacles he may have faced (in our case, having one arm injured). He went the extra mile by positively violating our expectancy, having built our *Sukkah* and caring for me.

Regardless of our religious or lack of belief, we should all strive to share the precious gift of love with each other just a little more. It costs nothing, and its return of investment is truly astronomical. This one-arm King serves as my role model for how to enliven and fulfill the essence of this holy law.

Legendary NBA coach Larry Brown would ask his players prior to each of their practices and games to choose one element of their game; passing, shooting, defense, hustle, it didn't matter, then to commit to him that they will improve that day in that field by just one percent. Each day, he would pose this challenge, leading his players to their eventual one hundred percent ability. I propose to you the same challenge. Commit yourself one percent more each day to loving your neighbor as you love yourself. You will be surprised how far it will take you, how much it'll give them and what adventures it will lead you towards.

Royal Food for Thought

- Before you begin to share the love, ask yourself, which person in your life would you like to show more love to? What new act will you commit to delivering towards them?
- What must you do to give the world that one more percent of yourself?

A Sheep in New Zealand

My 'desktop' adventure brought me countless lessons. However, it was my conversation with Roger about sheep that really got me thinking.

At times, we all wish to be worry-free and indistinguishable amongst the flock. But what does your life really hold then? Following my talk with Roger, I decided to sit one day amongst a woolly herd to reflect on what valuable lessons I can take from their presence and decided to write this poem.

A Sheep in New Zealand
By Doron Maman (October 22, 2014)

I wonder what it's like to be a sheep on the hill,
Who loves to eat grass and simply be still.
With no worries or threats about predators or pain,
Just to be one of the herd, just to be very plain.
Not asking questions; who, what, when or why?
Just to serve as a mirror for the clouds in the sky.
To be in New Zealand, part of the world's greatest view,
With no need for identity, not creating a who.
No competitions of beauty or strange-silly pageants,
It would then be so easy, to find eternal balance.
It seems like a dream, to great to be real,
But does this reality leave any room to feel?
We thrive for success and are always determined,
So when we overcome failure, we can deliver our sermon.
The pain, the struggles, the challenges and peaks,
Go up in our trophy rooms as memorable antiques.
We need these for life, we require them for growth,
All the emotions between, and a little bit of both.
So would I want to be a sheep in this picturesque desktop?
Or relieve my failures and climb back to the top?
These sheep are like dreams and are only temporary,
But when I'll stand on my hill, I'll be legendary.

Royal Food for Thought

- What valuable lessons can you take from creatures that are not humans? Choose any creature, study it and see what you can take from them to apply in your own life.

- My reflection on sheep allowed me to understand that my life is gifted by my challenges and how they have crafted my character. How have your struggles established you?

7

THE PETROL KING

"If a man is called to be a street sweeper, he should sweep streets even as Michelangelo painted, or Beethoven composed music or Shakespeare wrote poetry. He should sweep streets so well that all the hosts of heaven and earth will pause to say, 'Here lived a great street sweeper who did his job well.'"
-DR. MARTIN LUTHER KING JR.

I find the belief that contribution is dependent on one's position of power to be truly fascinating. We effortlessly overlook where and how we can be influential in our surroundings. This lesson hit home over the course of my BA in psychology.

Following the end of my military service, I decided to start a new path. I always loved partaking in great conversations and helping find perspective, so psychology seemed like the evident choice. I did not think about whether I would want to become a psychologist, I just sincerely believed in the importance of having these skills as a human being. Firstly, in order to learn the necessary cognitive skills to be mentally tough for myself, then for my loved ones, to know how to emotionally support them.

The studies were intense yet truly fascinating. I was being educated about the human mind and behavior like never before. Of all the courses, however, one particular class in social psychology struck me in a way that would have a major impact on my life. We were studying about the case of Kitty Genovese, a young American woman who was stabbed and murdered outside of her apartment building in 1964. While being attacked, she screamed for help as thirty-seven witnesses claimed to have seen or hear the occurrence. They all claimed that the reason they did not call for help was because they were sure that somebody else would do something. This phenomenon would later be coined in the world of social psychology as the 'bystander effect,' where people just stand by and do not take action as they feel there is a diffusion of responsibility.

A cool chill rattled through my bones as I initially thought to myself, *Not me! No way!* But the more I thought about it, the more apparent it became that maybe I too would also fall victim to this effect. And even more so, if we are all potential bystanders to such atrocities, we are all in danger!

Following this class, I took some time for personal reflection on what I had learned. Being so deeply disturbed by the detrimental possibilities, I made a conscious decision that day. I would not be the kind of student who absorbs material simply to pass exams, but rather I would search for daily opportunities to apply the gained knowledge beyond the classroom. Even more importantly, I would utilize various platforms to share my newly found lessons with as many people as possible. I sincerely believe that without application and transference, knowledge has no value. Applied knowledge becomes wisdom and we each must endlessly strive for this. I searched for opportunities to share this information, all the while continuously growing more perceptive.

Fortunately for me, I was already working in a wonderful organization as an instructor for youths, preparing them for their mandatory army service. I had three groups of over forty motivated high-school students from different cities. We would meet three times a week for highly strenuous physical training sessions simulating drills from a *gibush* and their future military service. I have always been a strong believer in leading by example, so I took advantage of every opportunity I could to get dirty and work hard with these students. These adrenaline-packed practices left us panting heavily and splashing the floor with sweat, but the content of the post-workout satisfaction was unparalleled.

As practices would come to a close, I would share about my service and various experiences. But I now recognized that this platform can allow me to provide so much more by incorporating a more value-based approach. I decided to change things up. As a cold winter practice came to an end, I asked, "How many of you have ever seen somebody being picked on at school?" Their faces lit up as they expected self-defense drills. Their hands rose immediately. "How many times have you seen somebody throwing trash in the street?" Again, the hands shot up, though slightly more confused. "Last question: What did you do about it?" We began to discuss the power of the bystander effect and what is needed to overcome it. None of them expected to come to train for the army by discussing psychology.

With time, however, this became my training trademark ritual. Each session concluded with me sharing theories, ideas and concepts from the worlds I was studying. My goal was to expose them to influential values and theories that would guide them towards firstly becoming excellent individuals, and only then, great future soldiers. These discussions were tagged as "Doron's Psychological Corner," and it became an inseparable part of my practices, all the while keeping me motivated to study in order to further contribute.

During the summer holiday, we organized special Friday morning practices on the beach at 07:00 A.M. which most of the students would attend. It is truly a one-of-a-kind experience to begin the weekend sprinting up and down a beautiful shore with a group of more than eighty energetic teenagers. Most teens do not recognize the sun on account of the fact that they are not usually up at these hours. But now they were having the time of their lives along with a weekly dosage of value from my psychological corner.

As I got up one Friday morning, I saw that I missed my alarm clock and was running late. I grabbed my shoes, sprinted down to the car barefoot and attired myself while driving. "Bing. Bing. Bing. Bing." My car began beeping obnoxiously, indicating that the gas tank was close to empty. I became concerned that my car would get stuck on the way and just managed to pull into a gas station.

I drove up to the gas attendant whom was firmly standing post at his position. "Good morning, how can I help you today sir?" the attendant asked with a kind voice. He was a short and chubby looking fellow with thick black hair wearing a red shirt with black and brown oil stains all over it. You could see by the black smudges on his hands that he was a hard worker.

"I just need to fill up. I'm in a bit of a rush."

"No problem sir." He sprinted around the car and opened the gas tank, placing the nozzle in. I kept looking at my watch hoping that the youths waiting for me would not leave. As the gas pumped, without any instruction or request, the attendant began to meticulously clean my rearview window, windshield and side mirrors. I knew I had the tendency to neglect the cleanliness of my car, but this was no time for a car wash.

I anxiously tapped the steering wheel, bouncing up and down in place hoping he would finish already. As the pump finally came to a stop, I looked to see where the attendant was. He was rolling large cleaning towel papers to thoroughly clean my windows. As he did so, he collected tons of dirt scraping off dried white and brown bird droppings that were sporadically scattered. "Sorry, but I really have to go!" I urgently said.

"Just one more minute," he asked. "Would you like me to check your oil and water levels?"

I was not used to getting this kind of quality service and did not even have the money to tip him. "No, I really have to go!" I truly could not wait a moment longer.

After another ninety-seconds of waiting, I finally paid him and rushed out of the station towards the beach. I regrettably knew I was breaking the speed limit, and managed to make it to the practice just several minutes late to find my students patiently waiting. We immediately got to work in what was an intense practice that included sand dune climbing, sprints and a month's worth of pushups. My heart rate finally slowed down as I soundly delivered my psychological corner.

It was another unequivocally great Friday morning practice, the kind that leaves both your muscles and thoughts fully satisfied. As I got back in the car to drive home, I suddenly saw a reflection of the transparently blue Mediterranean Sea through my extremely clean windows. I could not recall seeing the water glisten like that for quite some time, probably because of how dirty my car windows usually were. I took a moment to practice mindfulness as I gazed upon the view, while taking some deep calming breaths. I drove back home with a soft smile on my face, ready to begin my weekend.

A month later, when summer vacation was almost over, I was preparing to instruct another epic Friday morning beach practice. I had learned my lesson from a month ago and already inspected my gas level the night before. I saw I was missing more than enough and decided to get up a bit earlier in order to fill up on the way.

I pulled up to the station, this time in no rush. I instantly recognized the gas attendant who had served me previously. "Good morning, how can I help you today sir?"

Déjà vu. "Just to fill up on gas, thanks."

As soon as he placed the nozzle in the car, he immediately went back to cleaning the car as he had done a month prior. Wiping down the windshield, cleaning the rear-view window and every invisible speck in between. I did not really think my car needed to be cleaned this time, but whatever.

He removed the nozzle, closed the cap and collected the payment. "Thanks for choosing our gas station," he said in a polite tone. "I also just wanted to apologize for a month ago. I remember you were in a rush, but your windows were dangerously dirty. I couldn't take the responsibility knowing that it may lead to an accident." Talk about applying the bystander effect at a whole different level!

My jaw hit the floor. "How did you... how did you remember that?" I stuttered. He wiped down the summer sweat dripping from his forehead as he responded, "It's my job. I strive to provide excellent service because I know that even as a gas attendant, I can help people have a great day." I listened with genuine fascination as he continued. "I remember you were in a rush and I really wanted to provide the best service possible. So again I apologize. Have a safe drive." He smiled.

In pure amazement, I got out of the car to shake his hand, "You have no idea the power of what your service gave me. With that said, I have no idea what your service allows you to give to others." I looked at his heart through his eyes. "What's your name?"

"Oren." He replied humbly.

"I'm Doron, it's great to properly meet you. First of all, thank you for the excellent service, you're a truly special character. Secondly, can I take a picture of you?" As he tried to shy away, he finally complied. As we parted ways, I immediately knew I had met a uniquely humble King who served both his nation and their vehicles.

Throughout the entire practice, all I could think about was Oren's service. As I approached the psychological corner, I decided to share my experience from that morning rather than my usual theoretical knowledge. Upon concluding, I invited the high-school students the next time they or their parents had to fill up to stop by and ask for Oren to see first-hand what exceptional service is all about. After the practice, I shared the photograph on Facebook, telling my story about what I was privileged to receive that morning.

I did not fill up on gas the whole week so I could meet Oren again to get inspired before practice, to benefit from his unparalleled service and drink from his cup of humble knowledge. I pulled up to his station and promptly got out of the car to shake his hand. "Good morning Oren." I felt the oil from his hands rub off on to mine, hoping that his willingness to deliver unprecedented service would rub off as well.

I could tell by the firmness of his handshake that he was particularly excited to see me. "Doron, it's great to see you." He instinctively opened the cap of the tank, placing in the nozzle while holding our conversation. "I have to share something with you. This whole week, different people have been coming up to me, telling me that you told them to ask for me."

I smiled providing the only response I could. "Great people deserve great service. You know how to deliver that best."

To this day, unless I have no other option, I insist on filling up at Oren's post. Sometimes I will arrive and he will not be there, so I simply leave and return later that day, hoping to fill my car with gas and my spirit with excellence. It always amazes me to see how Oren's station always has a long line of vehicles waiting to be attended by him alone. It seems that I am not the only one who has benefited from the Petrol King.

Share Your Knowledge, Live Your Wisdom

There is a genuine desire in the world to acquire knowledge and gain wisdom. In order to do so, the information we learn must be shared and relayed onwards. Each person in our lives comes from different disciplines and has mastered certain skills and attributes that are authentically unique to them. Yet the skill we have each acquired remains meaningless if it does not serve a purpose. If an individual chooses to keep these skills, knowledge and values to themselves, it shall die with them. We each bear an exclusive philosophy which defines our lives and through its application, we attain various levels of wisdom.

Therefore, our responsibility is to always be on the lookout, ready and waiting for the opportunity to provide our essence to the world, while simultaneously craving to learn from those around us.

Selfishly keeping this knowledge to ourselves and not looking to make any form of contribution leaves us exposed to becoming potential victims of the bystander effect. Even if you do not know what your purpose is or what skill you have mastered (or yet to master), you must always be in movement, attempting to develop and strengthen yourself and your surrounding environment. Be patient. It will come.

In Phil Jackson's book *Sacred Hoops*, he shares about his experiences coaching the GOAT (Greatest of All Time), Michael Jordan. He shares how Jordan would dazzle the spectators while blowing his opponents away with his athleticism, creativity and competitive greatness. But it was all for nothing until Jordan understood that a championship would only come by making his fellow players better. Jackson would tell Jordan, "You've got to share the spotlight with your teammates because if you don't, they won't grow." This shift in focus raised the skill level of the team and eventually led to two three-peat championship runs.

We too should work in a similar fashion. By striving to make those around us better, we make ourselves and our surrounding environments even more exceptional. Bring the knowledge you have acquired to life by practicing and sharing it with others in your circle, believing that it will find its way to serve the world in perfect fashion. Share your knowledge, live your wisdom.

Royal Food for Thought

- What knowledge do you have to share with others to help them grow?
- What must you do to lead by example and thereby "live your wisdom?"
- How can you further apply your knowledge to become a wiser King or Queen?

Pump with the Purpose of Excellent Service

The great civil rights leader, Mahatma Gandhi, once said, "The best way to find yourself, is to lose yourself in the service of others." Answering the greater call of providing excellent service goes beyond trying to squeeze an extra buck out of your client. It is about allowing your essence to shine through all your actions, allowing everyone to grow and benefit. That is it! There is no higher purpose or calling in this world.

Oren did not just fill up my gas tank: he also made it his responsibility to deliver his best, through what appears to most as a mundane and overlooked profession. He made pumping gas a meaningful experience more so than a routine task. His excellent service is driven by asking powerful questions such as, "How can I make her drive more enjoyable? What can I do to make sure his car will experience less trouble? How can I improve the safety of this person's drive?" Could you imagine how extraordinarily we would live if we dedicated time to asking ourselves such questions each morning? We would consistently examine any and every opportunity to leave our mark on the world.

There is no need to be a brilliant detective to discover the influential impact of excellent service and its contribution to your personal brand. The real power, however, lies in the hidden and humble strength of acting so passionately. Oren never knew of my search for royalty, but his determination to provide all he serves with his very best inspired me to administer my very best to others. I have no doubt that this effect has rippled onto others as well.

It is thanks to Oren that I understand that one's purpose does not only become felt when doing what we love, but rather it shines through all of our actions and communications with people. It can be something universally influential or something as ordinary as pumping gas, but strive to leave your mark. This way, we further guarantee our immortality in this world by just sharing and dispersing bits and pieces of ourselves in the hearts of all we touch.

Royal Food for Thought

- Is there a King or Queen whose contribution you have over looked because they are not in a position of power? What will you now take from them?

- Minor contributions such as expressing gratitude, picking up trash or any other overlooked act can have monumental positive effects. What minor action will you commit to doing to further calibrate your personal royalty?

Leave a Car Better Than You Found It

As a kid, my teachers would consistently share their cleanliness mantra with our class, until we sang it in perfect harmony. "Keep your environment clean. Always leave a place better than you found it." However, only following my meeting with Oren and my time delivering my psychological corner did the true meaning of this quote become apparent. You see, it is not about leaving a place better than you found it, it is about leaving people better than you found them.

Sharing who we are through our values and essence via our daily actions and interactions can have global influences and impressions. What appears to be a humble ripple of thought can actually create a powerful tsunami of change! Think about all the greatest leaders throughout history from all disciplines. Have you ever asked yourself who influenced them? Generally, the answer is not someone who was as powerful as they were. But at some point in their lives, somebody told them something that would revolutionize their values and thought process. Somebody left them better than they were before. These characters of influence may have been parents, celebrities or maybe a local gas attendant, but by consistently applying this standard, you potentially and humbly enshrine your mark on the world while learning from those who surround you.

Every car that passes through Oren's station leaves better than it arrived. This is because above and beyond the excellent service the vehicle is provided with, the driver is now refueled with a personal example of what it means to act exceptionally. The magic of this type of fuel is that it may just drive the person to find a source of inspiration on how they too can become an extraordinary individual through each of their actions.

Royal Food for Thought

- What small change is required from you to leave people better than you found them?
- Define excellence. How does it differ from doing something 'excellently'? How will you apply this difference in your daily actions?

8

EAT MY GRATEFUL DUST!

"I either win or I learn."
-NELSON MANDELA

Nothing is more appealing to an IDF soldier than their 'legendary' release from the military and attaining well-earned freedom. After being fully immersed into an intense system, performing endless tasks under strict time constraints along with the constant uncertainty of what the following days hold, freedom appears to be a mysterious and untouchable creature that lurks in the darkness. It even becomes heartbreaking to fully accept that beyond the three years of mandatory service, is a world of new opportunities and adventures to be conquered. My fellow comrades and I use to joke about what it would be like to have more than one shower a week or what it would be like to go to sleep while it is dark outside and wake up to see the sun rather than the moon again (meaning we only slept three hours). Yet through it all, after three physically, emotionally and mentally draining years, in what seemed like an almost miraculous process like Moses splitting the sea, we successfully completed our service to become free men.

I walked past the tile covered fences headed towards the sunset for the final time like a cowboy in the final scene of a classic western film. As my mental credits began to roll, recognizing the influential characters that played in this film, I reflected on all that I have gained and learned towards my new awaited life. My main takeaway; freedom is not free, it must be earned. We only gain an appreciation for freedom (and for anything for that matter) after having lost it. We only become thankful for our health when we are sick. We only recognize the companionship of a loved one when they are gone. And until the day comes that you must forfeit your freedom in the name of a greater cause or due to an unfortunate circumstance, you never are truly aware of its presence and presents. This newfound power to act and speak as I desired had now become my most precious gift.

However, despite the glory of liberation, I never expected how such an immediate sense of independence can also be a threat to my character. I was no longer the meaningful fighter who protects others; gone was the spiffy uniform demonstrating my ranks like a proud peacock. And no longer would I be restricted to operating based on what I was told to do. Without new boundaries, this freedom could potentially become my downfall, leading me in erroneous directions. I was in need of a powerful purpose to guide my personal compass towards a new and meaningful direction.

I spent my days going on long runs (where my best thoughts come) and journaling to discover my driving values so that I could purposefully deliver my essence to others. I stood in place and reflected back on my life, anxiously looking forward towards the uncharted until it finally hit me; my purpose in life was to lead a life of significance and purpose. Although that seems to be extremely vague, this mindset had an overwhelming effect on what to search for in my environment. I searched for the ideal habitat in which I could establish this purpose and leave my mark on others. And as if I was struck by a moment of genius, the answer became immediately evident.

The following day, I applied for a job as an instructor for high-school students who were training for elite units in the IDF. During high-school, I was also a student in this organization and knew how significant it was for me. Recognizing the skills, attributes and understandings I had gained during my service, I became determined to deliver my purpose through this platform in which I felt my contribution would be greatest. I jumped into these waters with great certainty, simultaneously instructing three different groups in my first year. The levels of fulfillment and contribution were through the roof and I became addicted to this drug-like experience, only in search for more possible ways that I could deliver my personal touch. Beyond the physical elements of the practice (sand dune climbing, calisthenic exercises, long distance stretcher runs), I found a genuine platform in which I could inject values of mental toughness and personal excellence into the mindset of these youths. Over the next six years, I worked intimately in the organization, instructing over a thousand high-school students in yearly programs, became the head of the instructing team and genuinely pursued my passion of mentally training through various seminars I would conduct for the groups.

Through this line of work, I encountered countless different young Kings and Queens whom have provided me with groundbreaking lessons that have molded my character. However, it was not until my second-to-last year that I discovered amongst these royalties a King among Kings.

One beautiful Friday summer morning, we were preparing by the shore for a legendary beach workout. The eighty teenagers would show up at 06:45 A.M. to get ready and pumped for the awaited challenge. I greeted each with a customary high five and brotherly hug until I suddenly saw a new and unfamiliar face. He was a young skinny teenager with glasses and dark hair. You could tell he had experience in running just based on the thickness of the veins bulging from each of his legs. He approached me with a smile that ranged from ear to ear. "Hi my name is Assaf. I'm really excited to be here, I came to join the program. Thank you."

"Slow down, man." I responded with a chuckle. "I'm happy you came, but before you join, why don't you first try finishing the practice?" This morning's practice was an extremely challenging one as it coincided with one of our monthly challenges. It was a forty minute race in which the goal was to perform as many rounds as possible. One round consisted of twenty sit ups, then fully submerging into the salty sea, sprinting out to the shore to perform twenty clean chest-to-ground pushups and lastly a six hundred foot climb to the peak of an inclined sand dune. There were no breaks, and whoever completed the most rounds was declared the winner.

At a personal level, these practices were my opportunity to make my actions louder than my words and lead by personal example. Therefore, any opportunity to get in on these races, I wanted in! Why bark orders like you would at a dog when you can run with the pack? "The challenges I set for you are the same I set for myself." I told them as they gathered closely. "Let's do this!"

It was very rare that I would not win these races as I was usually the most mentally fit participator. Throughout the year I would consistently remind the students, "I guarantee you all three things. Number one: I am not the fastest person here. Number two: I am not the strongest person here. Number three: I am the mentally toughest son of a gun here, and that attribute is enough to win any battle!" My mental game was on and that was all I needed to achieve competitive greatness.

The race began and I started in my usual position, last. I incrementally began passing racers, one by one. Within four minutes, I comfortably established my position as the leader, or so I thought. I suddenly saw Assaf two hundred feet ahead. I could not let this new kid win, not on his first day. I had to catch him! I turned on the turbo and battled to close the distance but fell short as he would be declared the victor. I felt unaccustomed to the silver medal position on the podium. My head was hung low desperately trying to intake sufficient amounts of oxygen. As I forcefully inhaled, I felt a hand on my left shoulder blade and turned to see Assaf with the same smile he had prior to the race. "Wow, that was great!" he said in an exhilarating tone. Aside from the sweat stains on his chest, he looked as if he had not even moved a muscle. "Thank you for the competition. I was sure you'd catch me. See you next practice!" Still gasping for air, I simply raised my hand, giving a thumbs-up while nodding my head.

By the next practice, Assaf had already enrolled for the yearly program. Over the next year, we would compete with one another in epic races which always concluded in the same two ways: I would be his runner-up and he would then thank me for the competition. I was able to live with second place considering that I went to war pushing my limits against decent competition, but the "thank you" always confused me.

His mindset of gratefulness extended far beyond our competitions. It seemed as if his mind was set to an automatic response to anything that happened by humbly replying "Thank you." Not a single workout, competition, phone call, hangout or meeting ended with any other words. There was even a time when I needed technical help filling out long (boring) excel forms (which all instructors hated to do). He graciously took the extra assignment from me with his trademark response. I could not understand how somebody takes on extra work with such an appreciative demeanor. It began to bother me! Was this some sarcastic form of reverse psychology? If I was to receive somebody else's responsibility, I would be quite frustrated having to pick up their slack.

As the months passed we approached one of the main events of the year, "The Mother Nature Challenge." This annual six mile race is composed of various obstacles such as; army crawls, rope climbing, running through a forest, climbing sand dunes, entering and exiting the sea and a final climb up a severely angled six hundred foot street. In order to finish this ultimate race, the students would have to give their all. A first-place finish meant that you delivered your 'A game' like never before, pushing yourself in a truly phenomenal way.

With over one hundred and twenty athletically fit students prepared to participate, we decided to divide the competitors into two separate race times. The first would be in the morning and the second in the afternoon. This would allow the students to cheer each other on while their friends were racing and also to be cheered on as they would compete.

I was overlooking the morning session and excited to see the time that Assaf would put up knowing he would smoke the competition. In Assaf like fashion he blazed through the obstacles, penetrated through the water and left an appetizing trail of grateful dust for his competitors to feast on as he crossed the finish line setting a new course record: 52:17. For the first time in my memory, Assaf fell to his back gasping for air just fifteen feet past the finish line. He had put forth a truly worthy effort. As he dabbed the floor with sweat, I jumped to his aid and congratulated him. "That was awesome! Are you okay?"

As his stomach rapidly inflated and deflated while breathing, his eyes remained tightly shut. All he managed to do was quietly whisper into my ear "Thank you… Thank you…" I was not sure who he was thanking, but I laughed and picked him up. After several minutes, together we cheered on the remaining competitors. I later joked with him that he was lucky that I did not compete or he would have had to run even harder. He responded by saying, "I would have liked that."

I returned home that morning thinking, *That was insane!* It is very rare to see a person reach their maximum capacity (in any discipline). I mean literally doing everything in their physical and mental capacity just to achieve their absolute best. It was inspiring. As these thoughts planted their seeds in my mind, I became intrigued about our discussion. *What if I did compete against him?* I asked. *Had I raced, would I have been able to get to that point where my mental and physical efforts were on par with one another, delivering my greatest run yet?* As the seeds of these thoughts began to blossom, I reflected upon the wise words of a famed Chinese proverb, "The best time to plant a tree was twenty years ago. The second-best time is right now."

I still had an opportunity to discover. I decided that I was going to participate in the afternoon session. I mentally began to prepare myself by listening to my 'Marathon Man' playlist, pumping my blood with electrifying tunes like the rocking Foo Fighters song 'The Pretender', and the bass-pumping Kanye West song 'Power'. I knew my mind would have to be sharper than ever in order to bring my body to its maximum ability. I began to envision movies where I would see myself crossing the finish line as I ascended the final climb. I kinesthetically felt the pure satisfaction as if my efforts were reflective of a perfect score. I was preparing for something big.

I arrived to the afternoon session (despite not being scheduled to overlook it) dressed casually in jeans, running shoes and T-shirt. The competitors were stretching and were surprised to see me thinking I had simply come to cheer them on. I saw Assaf amongst a group of spectators crowded around the starting line. He too was casually dressed wearing sandals, jeans and a sleeveless shirt. We greeted each other as he shared with me his experience from the morning's race.

The organizing instructor abruptly called out, "Racers to the starting line." As the group of sixty competitors prepared themselves, I left Assaf jumping into the middle of the pack. I took off my jeans revealing my running shorts. The students and instructors became surprised to discover that I was joining the race and responded with cheers and hollers. I was the only instructor participating and I could not be more excited.

The countdown began as we all chanted together, "Five…four… three…two…one… go!" As the whistle blew, I opened my stop watch and began to sprint down the shore. I never opened a race this fast but I had a clear goal, to deliver my absolute best in every sense. As I launched myself head-first into the sea like a piercing torpedo and army crawled out, I moved on to the sand dunes. I occasionally leaned on to my hands to assist my feet as I was already being weighted down by the water and the heavy sand I collected in my shoes. I pushed harder believing with every cell in my body that I could enliven the images I created in my mind. My musical playlist looped in the back of my head, only escalating my adrenaline. I had no idea whether there was anybody behind me or not, nor did I care. I was completely committed to the present, focusing on defeating my greatest competitor – my shadow.

I continued to run until the sand dune led me into the forest area where I cut through the trees like a predator in the culmination of his hunt. My prey was in sight and I was starving! I arrived to the rope climb, ascending the fifteen-foot obstacle like a modern-day Tarzan playing on a tree vine. There was no room for thinking about being weak or strong. It was all about doing my best and so I did. I climbed down the rope and returned towards the shore for my final obstacle, the street climb.

At this point, this final ascent appeared nothing short of Mount Kilimanjaro. My leg muscles burned as my lungs were about to implode. But worst of all, my mind became invaded with brigades of voices justifying reasons to slow down. *Doron! Nobody is behind you, and you did such a good job. Just relax, take it easy. You may also want to run this weekend, so don't burn yourself out. Wave to the spectators, take your time.* As the thoughts kept coming, I had a choice to make: surrender or pursue the true meaning of "give it your all."

I closed my eyes, bit my bottom lip and started leaving mental skid marks on the road behind. With only two hundred feet left, I recognized Assaf at the finish line. As he cheered me on with the other spectators, he kept looking at his watch. "Faster Doron, faster!" With one hundred feet to go, my arms and legs perfectly synchronized to establish the needed momentum. "Just a few more steps!" As the street came to an end, I crossed the line, stopped my watch and caved into the floor, also now dabbing the street with my own pools of sweat.

The observing students surrounded me as they picked me up to my feet. I felt my body in a way that I had not felt since I was back in the army. Although my legs felt as if they were made of jelly, my mind was at ease. I knew that I delivered my absolute best. This was the feeling of victory I envisioned.

I desperately gasped for air while Assaf bestowed upon me a brotherly hug. "That was awesome," he said.

I fell back down to my knees as I managed to mumble, "You were…you were… my inspiration." I slowly collected myself. "I just wanted…." Inhale, exhale. "To do it like you."

"I think you did better." He laughed as he extended his left arm towards my face. "Check out your time."

For the first time since the race began, I looked at my watch. 52:09. I was in shock. I had finally beaten him. Although this was always a goal of mine, I was thankful to be riding a mental high knowing that I had achieved an elated peace of mind. By peace of mind, I mean a state in which I could walk away from the experience knowing that I did everything in my power to achieve success. For me, this is more powerful than any record of any kind.

As I hugged the young King, I collapsed into his arms as my legs remained wobbly. We laughed together, as I told him, "Thank you man. That was awesome."

The Never-Ending Thank You

Assaf's unrelenting attitude of gratitude was truly like none I had ever encountered before. This youthful King managed to master a mindset in which he was untouchable to the world, as he remained thankful for all that came his way. I believe the key word here is "all," as he truly was grateful for every single thing. He sincerely embraced the good, the bad and the ugly with an unshakable love and appreciation.

I believe he maintained this because of his understanding of a fundamental law of life; everything will always work itself out! All challenges are possibilities in disguise, which eventually come to serve us. Until this day, he acts with the belief that in the end, everything will always be perfect, and if it is not perfect, it is simply not the end. The key difference between Assaf and most of us is that the rest of us wait to say thank you until we see the value we have gained. He expects the eventual arrival of the value and therefore delivers his appreciation prior to its appearance. He consciously leaps over the stage of strife and mental strain, and patiently awaits for the landing of the lesson.

This understanding is further reflected in his authentic expression of acknowledgement for competition. Every time we laced our shoes and raced, he would genuinely express appreciativeness for our rivalry. I found this so strange because you rarely see tier one competing athletes tell one another, "Thanks for almost beating me. You made my training a living hell!" Assaf, however, understood that only when we are surrounded by excellent adversaries who challenge our position to ascend the summit, will we strive for a new level of personal peak performance. His thankfulness in this sense was motivated by his desire to continue to better himself as a runner and as a person. It is an amazingly humble trait that allows for optimal drive.

Thank you, Assaf, for this awe-inspiring lesson.

Royal Food for Thought

- What challenging opportunities in life are you currently not expressing gratitude for?
- How would you perceive and act on them differently if you were already grateful for them?

Remember, You Are Human!

In ancient Greece, the Olympics would celebrate athletes in various sports, creating a platform that allowed them to compete and discover who was master and champion of their discipline. Winners would stand in front of a roaring crowd and have laurels placed upon their head by a spectator whom they truly trusted. As the leaf crown was bestowed on the head of the respected champion, it was customary to quietly whisper into the ear of the athlete, "Remember, you are human."

Assaf had beaten me more times than I could possibly count, but he returned to each practice more driven than the previous. Rather than standing boastful atop his mountain of collected victories whilst inflating his ego, he remained passionately hungry for more. He maintained his focus on 'poise' rather than 'pose' just by remembering that he is human. The Greeks knew that the most important time in the careers of the athletes to have them recall their mortality was during their glorious moments of victory. This encouraged athletes to continue to passionately engage in sport with great respect and humility, striving to deliver and discover new personal bests – becoming comfortable in the illusory and non-existent throne of success, will never lead to further progress. The only subsequent step from here is decline.

In the critically acclaimed film *Whiplash* (2014), a promising young drummer who aspires to become the greatest percussionist of his time is guided by his overly strict mentor. As they reflect on the radical methods previously applied by the instructor, the teacher shares an interesting notion with his prodigy. "There are no two words more harmful in the English language than 'good job.'" Although the approach is quite extreme, there is a powerful underlying essence here. It says that we should always strive to learn where to improve, never accepting that we have attained perfection. As legendary NFL coach Vince Lombardi once so masterfully said, "Perfection is not attainable, but if we chase perfection we can catch excellence." Remembering that we are human establishes an endless pursuit after such excellence whilst maintaining the most authentic humility.

No matter who Assaf was racing, he enthusiastically engaged in competitive wars, hunting for new possibilities that would allow him to achieve his own personal bests. Enjoy the crisp air at the peak of your success. Just remember that tomorrow holds new chances to develop your craft and although you are now a champion, remember you are still human.

Royal Food for Thought

- Do you humbly continue to learn and develop the craft in which you have championed or have you remained stagnant in your dim faded glory?
- What additional acts can you take to continue advancing in the field you have mastered?

Race Your Shadow

We live in a world that initially claims to appreciate and recognize individual efforts, yet places a greater emphasis on delivering results. Such results are generally determined and compared to the social world and standards set by others. This occurs because as we grow up, we are taught by multiple social platforms that if you are not first, you are not remembered. That you must be better than everybody else and it is not enough to continuously better yourself.

Most people claim that they are the outliers who praise the efforts of others and are not the victims of this dominating matrix. In the case that you are amongst these chosen ones, allow me to test you with a question. Who is the fastest man in the world? If you are at all familiar with the world of sports, you probably confidently answered Usain Bolt, and you would be correct (as of the 2016 Olympics). But now answer this. Who is the second-fastest man in the world? Of the thousands of people I have asked in my lectures and travels across the globe, the majority cannot even provide any kind of answer! Even more so, the lecture halls are usually flooded with the chirps of crickets as nobody has even the slightest clue. This is because we have all been programmed throughout life to only vacate enough mental storage for whoever is number one (as of the 2016 Olympics, the second fastest man is Justin Gatlin).

However, just because this thought process has been forced upon us, does not mean that it is right or that it is too late to remove ourselves from it! If we are aware of our tendency of falling prey to this fallacy, we should correctly orient ourselves with the beliefs and values we see fit. For me, these values are reflected by consistently racing my own shadow. This means that rather than determine my level of success in comparison to that of another, I recognize that as long as I am putting forth my greatest possible effort, I am producing my greatest possible result and that is true success. Racing your shadow is reflected in having an endless commitment: that you strive each day to become better than you were the day before.

If I determine my growth and development in comparison to someone else, I will grow accordingly with them and possibly give up the chance to fulfill my ultimate potential. By using yourself as a measuring stick and consistently focusing on improving your previous performance, you will experience true and humble growth while mastering your discipline.

At the end of the day, the only person I am competing with is myself. If I can be a better Doron today than I was yesterday, then victory will become imminent.

Royal Food for Thought

- Whose standard have you set for yourself in your discipline? Are you trying to be better than yourself or somebody else?
- Try and recall a time in which you raced against yourself and won. How do you compare this personal victory to that of overcoming another?

9

CHEERS TO WORK!

"If opportunity doesn't knock, build a door."
-MILTON BERLE

Human beings tend to act out of a certain urgency to get things done. We feel the need to see and try as much as possible and as soon as possible rather than fully savor the present flavors. We are driven to possess the most up to date technological devices before we have fully utilized the potential of our current one. While traveling, we are driven to exhaust all the attractions having seen each sight. Bottom line, we rush through the exhilarating thrill and power of the now, only to look back later in our lives wishing he had absorbed the experience in full.

This notion became apparent to me as I was reflecting on the life of my grandmother who had just recently passed. I looked back on the final twenty-five years of her life and thought, *How much variety did she experience? How many new things did she try?* The more I pondered, the more I realized that had she not rushed to complete so much at a young age, she still would have had so much to strive for in her final years. In the bigger picture of life, such an approach can simply be a straight-up game changer!

This insight led me to create my own personal bucket list which I called The Life List. I filled a large poster with close to one hundred different dreams, missions and goals I wished to perform prior to my death. I wanted to be really creative and wrote things like attending the World Cup finals, participating in the yearly Pamplona (running of the bulls in Spain), writing a book, becoming a motivational speaker, having coffee with Michael Jordan and many more.

In order to make sure that I did not sprint through this list and could truly appreciate each experience, I declared that my goal was to perform at least one task a year. I did not want just my five senses to enjoy the ride, I sincerely wanted to find and learn the added value hidden behind each adventure. Each experience in life (good or bad, easy or challenging) always holds more than what meets the eye, but only to those who search for its value. Searching for the values in between the lines of life leads us towards discovering new majestic Kings and Queens who bear empowering life lessons. Ultimately, we all come to the same finish line, looking back at all of the experiences we had, only to find what truly remains is the value and lesson we attained.

Amongst my listed tasks was to open my own business one day. In order to spend more time with my father while growing up, I would go to work with him in his warehouses on the weekends, just to take in some of his character. I would be introduced as the next "big boss," the future CEO. Each morning, he would greet each of his several hundred workers by name as he masterfully balanced between being the attentive ear and the authoritative power. Loved by his nation of workers like a magnificent Roman general, he was more than a typical boss. He was always respectful towards everyone, first recognizing the person and then the worker. As a juvenile studious bystander, I knew that I would follow in his footsteps one day and open my own venture. I was always intrigued by leadership, and seeing that I shared the genes of a man who handled people so admirably drove me to add this mission to my list.

"Where do I start? What do I do?" I asked. I did not really have a clear direction, but I knew that I wanted as much contact with people as possible. I wanted to learn and to teach, to lead and at times to follow, all the while having a positive effect on those around me.

I became frustrated thinking that there was no such business model, until I decided to make a call to a good friend, Daniel. Daniel and I had studied together during our BA and were also both featured TEDx speakers. He was a short skinny guy with glasses who was born and raised in Los Angeles. Always dressed to impress with his buttoned-down Bonobos shirts and spiffy getup, classmates would tag him as, "The one that was going places." He was always in the loop of everything happening in the business world and was even working in a quite successful start-up at the time. He led the business development of a company that created a portable printer about the size of a grown man's fist. During our studies, we would always entertain the thought that one day we would do something together. I decided to give him a call.

"Hey Daniel. It's Doron, what's up man?"

"Yo man!" he replied with his southern Californian accent. "What's going on?"

"Good bro. I've been thinking, I want to get into the business world. But I'm not sure what to…" Daniel interrupted before I could even finish my sentence.

"Do you want to be a co-founder in a start-up with me?" I was kind of shocked by his abruptness. It was like going out on a first date and before your drinks arrive, the girl asks you if you want to get married. "I've had this idea for a while and I really want to move on it. I just need a partner."

His energy had me hooked. "What did you have in mind?"

Daniel began telling me how he had been working out of a coworking space in New York for his start-up. If you are not familiar with the world of coworking, in recent years there has been a large movement of private businesses and freelancers sharing large, beautifully renovated workspaces, bringing the best of all worlds under one productive roof. Rather than paying astronomical prices to rent formal offices or invading various coffee shops daily, people use these beautifully designed spaces as their new office. Each day on his way to work, he would pass by newly refurbished bars that were closed during the day and sat untouched. "Why am I not I working from here?" he thought. This was the conceptual birth of a potential start-up: transforming bars that are only open at night into affordable and productive coworking spaces during the day.

"I'm still at my current job. I want to do this, but if I do, I need a full-time, hard-working partner and co-founder to build this idea from the ground up. Someone I can trust. What do you think?" he proposed.

I knew this would mean that I would also have to leave my job and expose myself to a whole new realm, one in which I had no experience. I smiled. "When are you free to meet?"

Over the next two months, Daniel and I got our hustle on and would work incredibly hard to bring this product to life. We would meet in Tel Aviv with our bikes and ride from bar to bar, pitching our idea to over thirty potential locations. We studied other coworking spaces and their business models to further understand the field. We both left our jobs and became full time parents to our new baby, which we named "The Pub Hub."

By the end of the two months, we were ready to officially launch our proof of concept in our first location in Tel Aviv. It was a poorly lit, two-floor bar with the stench of beer, not far from the beach. With our location set, it was time to really flex our 'hustle muscle'. Mornings would commence at 06:00 A.M. in order to clean the tables, move over one hundred bar stools outside and then connect our office equipment (printer, coffee machine, etc.). Once the venue was set, we created and pushed campaigns on social media, stormed coffee shops in search for potential customers, established partnerships with local businesses, gave free talks at events and universities and anything else to get our first customers in the door. And after four weeks of hustle and grit, long days and restless nights, we officially had four members. Not quite the number we were going for. Despite that, we still truly believed in our idea and were going to do anything we could to make it happen.

With the beginning of week five, I entered the (empty) Pub Hub to find Daniel staring at his computer through his glasses from point blank. I walked over to him and asked what was up. As his eyes remained glued to the screen, he responded. "Yo, I got this mail from a friend." He turned the computer screen towards me. "He thinks we should enter. What do you think?" I skim read the email reading that Credit Suisse (one of the world's most powerful banks) was holding its annual high-tech start-up competition and that we were invited to come and try out. Over eighty successful start-ups would apply and only the top five would be invited to present at a prestigious event to over two hundred international bankers and wealthy private investors. The winning start-up would win free legal counseling, a one-year internship with Credit Suisse and an all expense covered trip to London to present their start-up to a pool of extremely wealthy private investors in a private conference.

I chuckled as my eyes read over the prizes. "That's crazy man. But we're not even high-tech! We've got so much else to do…" I paused. "Actually, you know what? To hell with it, let's just have fun and see what happens." We spent the next two hours filling out all the relevant documents, then immediately got back to our work. We returned our focus to how we were going to get more people to join our coworking space.

Three days later, we received an email with the following subject line, "Congratulations, The Pub Hub has been selected for the semi-finals!" We opened together what we were sure was a prank mail only to discover that it was real! They asked to meet the team and invited us for a prolonged interview. As one of us always had to be physically present at the bar, we decided that Daniel should go to represent us. We still had no expectations of making it to the finals, since we were not high-tech, but again we laughed, "To hell with it. Let's just have fun."

As the week came to a close and our clientele numbers remained stagnant, we sat down to brainstorm for new marketing ideas. As we proposed new ideas, the table began vibrating as Daniel's phone was ringing on it. A restricted number. "Hello?"

"Hello Daniel, this is Susanne from the Credit Suisse Headquarters in Zurich." I could hear the politeness and formality of her voice through the earpiece glued to Daniel's head. "We are glad to inform you that The Pub Hub has been selected for the finals of the 2016 High-Tech Forum Pitching Ring. Congratulations!"

Daniel and I tried to keep our cool as we intermittently broke out into laughter. I placed my hands on my balding head in pure disbelief. All I could think was, *Do they know we only have four customers? Do they not understand that we are not high-tech?* This seemed like a satirical comedy, except that I was not sure who was the butt of the joke. Was it us or them?

Daniel paced back and forth as he continued to speak on the phone while I researched the previous years' competitions online. As he hung up, we felt a new electric flow of energy fill the dim unoccupied bar. Now, in addition to our usual work, we had a lot of preparing to do as we realized that this could be our big chance! Not that we thought that we had a chance to win, but maybe we would meet a potential investor or connection to help us launch this project off the ground. At the bare minimum, we would at least just have some fun.

Over the next week, we added to our daily schedule tasks such as reading articles, printing business cards and perfecting the four-minute pitch that Daniel would deliver on our behalf. Our competition was fierce, comprised of four other successful start-ups that had already received funding and had acquired hundreds of thousands of users. We were now officially entering the business coliseum as an immature David against four behemoth-like Goliaths!

The big day arrived. We dressed to fit the part and came several hours early to practice on the stage that Daniel would be delivering his pitch. Various stage managers and technicians were preparing the large stage which was placed in front of two hundred vacant seats. If you suffer from glossophobia (fear of public speaking), this definitely was not for you. Although Daniel was a great speaker, the pressure was on. "Yo man. Get on stage, feel it out." I told him.

Daniel stepped out into the spotlight and began running through his pitch. Every word was on cue, the text was spot on, but something was still missing. "Listen man. Its perfect! You've got this easy! Just add one more thing." I paused. "You've got to give them a piece of your heart – a piece of your passion. Let me ask you, why do you care so much about this project?"

Being the geeky sheik that he was, Daniel responded, "Cause I love connecting people. I love being a part of people's creative processes, helping them out."

I smiled, preparing for my cliché yet genuine moment. "That's what's missing! Your heart." I said while pointing to the left side of my chest. "Speak from there. The pressure will evaporate because it's just you and your passion. There are plenty of ideas out in the world that'll make investors billions of dollars. But there aren't many founders who pursue their business with such drive and conviction to bring others to a higher level. That's your value! That's our value! People just talk to these investors' logic and brains all day. Shake things up. Talk to their heart from yours. Say what you said to me and give that part of you to the listeners."

He exhaled releasing tension. "I'll give it a shot." One of the stage managers asked us to get off stage as the audience started to arrive. We took our spots and sat patiently as the opening remarks were made by various bankers and wealthy venture capitalists. I kept looking over towards Daniel who seemed more antsy than excited. If we were going to have any shot at this, we had to get Daniel excited and not nervous. Daniel was going to present to a prosperous crowd in thirty minutes, and although I blindly trusted his skills as a speaker, I wanted him to have the extra edge and to remind him to speak from his heart.

I ripped a small piece of paper from my binder and wrote him a small note with only seven words on it. As Daniel got up with the other four presenters to get mic'd up, I put the folded note in his hand. "Yo. Before you begin to talk, read this. You got this!" I could feel the jitters in his high five but had full faith in him.

We were presenting fourth which I found ironic considering we only had four members. The start-ups took stage one by one to deliver their pitch. As soon as I started hearing the numbers they were delivering, my hope for an upset began to wither. The first company presented their application, which gives small businesses unique user feedback, and claimed they currently had over a quarter million users. The second presented their algorithms, which help people save money looking for mortgages and recently exceeded one million users. The third venture worked with a database that relayed agricultural information to farmers from their plantation and had already been working with farms all over the country. These were undoubtedly some heavy hitters.

Daniel stood on deck, preparing to jump on stage. I signaled to him from the audience with loud, expressive body gestures, mouthing the words, "Open the note!"

As the third start-up received their applause for their presentation, Daniel reached into his pocket and opened the folded paper. It read, "To hell with it! Just have fun!" Daniel started to laugh as he gave the thumbs up.

He stepped right foot first into the spot light, grinning with excitement and began to persuasively deliver his charismatic message. "This is a thirty-billion dollar market… coworking spaces in the shared economy is the future…we are potentially the most scalable coworking company in the economy…" Daniel was on fire, impressively delivering his well crafted pitch. As he brought his case to a close, he was left with thirty-seconds, just enough time to add one final thing. "Before I finish, I'd just like to share something on a personal note." The mood in the venue changed. "My co-founder Doron and I love this. We love coming to work to help our loyal members create more. We believe this platform will help countless others to pursue what they are passionate about and we just hope to be the ones that assist them along their way. They deserve this. Thank you."

The crowd erupted in applause as Daniel humbly bowed and exited stage right. I waited behind the podium to embrace him with a royal hug as he came down. "That was awesome!" I told him, "Whatever happens, happens." We had both finally fully surrendered to the circumstances as we had no additional way to influence or control the decision. We laughed together knowing we had a blast, holding little to no concern regarding the outcome. As in the lyrics of the classic Jack Johnson song 'Times Like These', "What will be will be, and so it goes."

The final start-up then presented their app which connected professional musicians to one another, also displaying their numbers of the several hundreds of thousands of dollars they raised. And at last, the final whistle was blown. The decision now shifted into the audience's hands, as each member would receive an electronic remote with the numbers one through five. They would vote for the company they thought had the most potential by pressing the corresponding number of the start-up. The company with the most votes would win.

We congratulated the other presenting start-ups on having come so far with their product as the votes were tallied. We exchanged business cards and offered them our services if they were ever looking for a cool, new place to work from. If we were not going to win, then at least we might find some new customers.

"Ladies and gentlemen," a voice called from the speakers. "The votes have been registered and a winner has been selected." Daniel got back up on stage as the audience refocused their attention towards the MC. A curiosity of who would be victorious brewed in the venue. "The winner of the 2016 Credit Suisse High-Tech Forum Pitching Ring is…" I could hear the other start-ups biting their finger nails all the way from the audience. "The Pub Hub!"

"Whoa!" I yelled in pure disbelief. I immediately covered my mouth as not to scream again! Daniel walked up to the presenter to receive the trophy as we were embraced by a deafening applause. As the forum came to a close, we were interviewed by various journalists, Bloomberg TV and were congratulated by the audience and our worthy competitors. We left the venue victorious, feeling that we had conquered the world, ready to return to our four loyal members the next day.

Without a doubt, we both felt like Kings bringing home a glorious victory in the name of our newfound kingdom. After having achieved the unthinkable, these two Kings would get back to lifting chairs at their everyday hustle the next morning.

Everyday I'm Hustlin' (Humbly)

Although Daniel was small in stature, his 'hustle muscles' looked like that of the incredible hulk. His mind was sharp and his to-do list was endless. "There's always something we can be doing," he would say. "If you ever need something to do, just let me know." I would get calls from him during all hours of the day as his mind was always wrapped around the question, "What else can we be doing for this to create more value?"

This King-like mindset kept him consistently hunting for new opportunities, ideas and partnerships. He just gets it! He gets that getting your 'hustle' on means that you have done everything in your power to achieve success. Time and time again, Daniel would tell me, "We can be doing more!" More importantly, this attitude and approach only became enhanced after our victory in the competition and this is what makes his hustlin' attribute so notable.

However, what made his hustlin' approach so unique was that he would do so humbly. Despite the prestigious title of co-founder of a start-up, despite the glory that accompanies the victory of winning such a distinguished competition, he was always willing to do the dirty work. Lifting the chairs, scrubbing the floors and anything else needed to achieve success. He would strive to make every minute count, removing himself from his title, connecting to his passion and leading by example. For me, it was nothing short of inspirational to learn from this business King.

I believe that what separates the doers from the talkers is simply their ability to hustle. This extends beyond performing the work that they are familiar with, but their willingness to do whatever it takes to achieve success. Winners are not born at the top of the mountain. They have a clear understanding of where they came from and work hard to climb to the top. Once at the peak, they only work harder to stay there. That is what hustlin' (humbly) is all about.

We all have something that we wish to succeed in. Whether you want to ask out the girl of your dreams, succeed in your discipline or run a mile, just start hustlin'. Know that beyond the taste of victory that awaits you at the finish line, your hustle makes you a prime candidate to obtain grit based mental values such as discipline, mental toughness and courage. The glory of success is only intensified by the amount of hustle you put in. So get your hustle on, humbly.

> ## Royal Food for Thought
>
> - Analyze the steps you have taken to achieve your goal. Are you doing everything in your power to achieve success?
> - Write down one more thing you can be doing to get closer to victory.
> - What more can you do to create greater value for others?

The Sixth Sense

I cannot say for sure why we won the pitching ring, considering that we were such a long shot, but if I had to guess, it would be because Daniel presented not only our potential value as a company, but even more so our values as a team. Values which radiated that we genuinely care about our clients. That we hold our clients' success as our own and that we want to provide what we believe people deserve (affordable and productive work spaces).

The bottom line is that people always want more value! This is why we have value meals at fast-food restaurants, why commercials show us the additional value in the most up-to-date gadgets, why one company's membership is more valuable than their competitors. At the relational level, we endlessly search for friends who hold certain values to the highest standard which instill in us a belief that we can always rely on them.

Throughout our lives, we have become so focused on feeding our five senses with as many various forms of stimulation as possible that we rarely get to grasp what is it that we are truly taking away from the experience, and that is value. Value our sixth sense.

Unlike our other fleeting experiential senses, the sense of value is long lasting. As time expires, these values shift and form our character to become people of ideals, ethics and well-founded principles. Of all our six senses, this is the one we should be consistently striving to feed!

Recognize that every opportunity (without exclusion) provides us with a platform to give and take value from the world. When we tune our senses to look for them, we absorb and apply them within our own lives, thereby becoming more royal - like Kings and Queens. Furthermore, when others begin to appreciate that you strive to provide such value, they become captivated and intrigued. It is well known in the start-up world that investors are not just looking to invest in good ideas. They equally invest in the teams promoting them. Likewise in life, people invest in people. They invest energy into their discussions, they invest attention towards their relationships, and in the business world, they invest money into the team and their product. But only if they can reveal true value.

We all have values that we can give and can take from the world. This is the essential core belief of Breakfast with Kings. It is searching through life's experiences for all the hidden and added values. Let's take all of our direct and indirect relationships and aim to appreciate their value. Just as importantly as all of these, it is about discovering how we can share our value with the world, to become co-creators and co-workers.

Royal Food for Thought

- What are you doing to create more value for others both as a person and in your profession?
- What is your core essential value that you wish to share with all you touch?

To Hell with It, Just Have Fun!

Some experiences come once in a lifetime and I believe it is absolutely vital to fully enjoy them. The problem is, that at some point we shift our focus to the pressure at hand and almost entirely miss the thrill of the ride. The key notion we are overlooking here is that unless we embrace this tension, it will dominate us.

Throughout the entire process of the Pitching Ring (from our application to our presentation), Daniel and I redirected our focus from being victorious (a pressuring goal) to just enjoying the moment. To remind ourselves of this, we adopted the mantra "To hell with it, just have fun!" In order for us to fully relish in the experience at hand, we knew that there was a need to remove ourselves from stress and joyfully embrace the present. This reminds me of one of my favorite quotes from the film *Kung-Fu Panda* (2008), "Yesterday is history, tomorrow is a mystery. But right now is a gift, and that is why it is called the present."

We eventually all look back at our memories that were filled with mental strain and tell ourselves, "I wish I had more fun with that." We look forward with anxiousness to major events in our lives knowing we should tell ourselves, "Just let it come. You're not there yet." So if we know that these are the responses that wait at the end of the tunnel, why not just skip the strife and anxiety, and go straight to having fun? Whether you like it or not, this is a conscious choice that we can each make.

However, if you are still unable to remove yourself from the tensioning stress, all you have to do is go back to your heart just as Daniel did. This may sound cliché, but I sincerely believe that all the answers that we seek are inside of us. The bottom line is that at all times, you are always with you. All that you need to do to discover yourself, is just go to your heart and search for the answer. It's always been there. Put your hand on your chest, close your eyes and bravely ask yourself, "Why is this so important to me? Why am I doing this?" You will know the answer when it comes and when it does, fully connect to it, appreciate it and strap in, because you will begin to conquer whatever it is that you are facing with a smile on your face. You will become an active participant in creating an epic victory that you may have never thought was possible.

As the famed French philosopher Blaise Pascal so perfectly put, "The heart has its reasons of which reason knows nothing." Trust those reasons and go with all your heart.

Royal Food for Thought

- Look in retrospect at the event that you tagged as 'stressful'. How do you look back on it now? How do you think you would look back on it in five years from now?

- Go to your heart. Ask yourself, why is what you are doing so important to you? Write it down or say it aloud.

10

THE GARDENER, THE GRANDMOTHER AND MR. SEXY LEGS

"It is a curious thought, but it is only when you see people looking ridiculous, that you realize just how much you love them."
- AGATHA CHRISTIE

I was afraid. On one hand, I felt that I was conquering the world achieving admirable accomplishments, yet on the other, I remained dominated by a single fear, that I would never find my significant other and would remain companionless, never having that someone who I can celebrate my victories with. Ultimately, success is worthless if you have nobody to share it with. After countless unsuccessful relationships, I would spend my nights gazing at the stars, pondering "Is she out there? Does she even exist?"

But what was even more astonishing was that I was not alone. I learned that I was surrounded by people who were also anxious regarding whether they would find their compatible soul mate or not. Many of them remained paralyzed in fear just from the thought of approaching someone. Even the world's boldest warrior becomes as apprehensive as the cowardly lion from the Wizard of Oz when challenged to ask the girl sitting at his local coffee shop for her phone number.

The bottom line is that it takes balls to repetitively get back in the game of love, to overcome heartache, to crush the concerns of rejection and to remain vulnerably exposed. This is why so many people remain hesitant, because their logic is that if they do not play, they will not lose. Although that is true, if you do not play, you cannot win either and you therefore have no right to ask the question, "Where's the love of my life?" He will not arrive on a galloping steed calling your name from under your window. She will not message you on a Saturday night on Facebook asking, "Would you like to take me out for dinner?" If you want it, you are going to have to work.

After countless attempts, I had been shattered by so many women that I could no longer keep track. I tortured myself to portray the ideal man I thought every woman would want. An attractive debonair who was, kind, funny and confident. I became less of myself and more emotionally invested in each relationship. Over time, I became depressed on account that when a former lover would leave, I would feel she was taking hard-earned parts of me with her, and that I would never get them back. I felt physical pain as if I was parting from myself longing for a phantom limb. Although learning to deal with this became easier, it was never easy.

As I progressively separated from more fragments of myself, I became frightened that nothing would remain. I grew worried as I did not know how I could completely give myself to another, if I had nothing left to give. It was not until my mother reminded me of an old enlightened adage that I understood how to move forward. "A tree that does not receive water cannot give any fruit." This fundamental principle claims that if you do not focus and invest in yourself, then you cannot devote yourself to others. It is about first becoming your own best friend, owning and developing the skills to support, love and accept yourself at all times. After this, you will be able to serve your majestic Queen or King with endless fruit to reap from.

The approach I held until now had me deceiving myself at the beginning of each relationship as I strayed further from my values and character to embody what I believed my potentially significant other would want. But this fruit-giving tree philosophy gave me a more profound perspective. That even if I did manage to find a partner, by maintaining this facade, I would be deceiving both her and myself. She would discover a different individual whom she did not really fall for, and I would lose the essence which I worked so hard to establish. The latter deception appeared to be far more consequential for both sides.

I strategically refocused myself within in order to initially become my own most loyal and trusted ally – to know that in all times of need, I can firstly rely on my being there for myself and that in moments of triumph, I can joyously reward myself with a celebratory high five. I rebuilt my character from the ground up, applying all the precious lessons that I gained from each of my failed relationships. I rid myself of my victim status to become a curiously humble student of virtue. I was refocused on growing into the shoes of a better man, firstly for myself and only afterwards for my future companion.

With this new mindset, I now asked a new question that encouraged both personal integrity and space for relational growth. "What three values will I not bend on?" This question established a non-deceptive platform that would reconnect me to my core beliefs. If a potential partner slightly deviated from any one of these ideals, then I simply knew that we were not meant to be and that was fine.

However, if she successfully answered all three criteria, then I would commit to learning and accepting all of her qualities that did not coincide with mine. Such sincere acceptance would allow for endless growth for both parties as we would take in from each other's essence and knowledge.

Finding and sustaining a meaningful relationship is completely reliant on our ability to accept and learn from the other. It seems to me that so many people want their life partner to be a perfect match in their characteristics and preferences, rather than receive a person who more so completes them. I mean the kind of person whose distinctive attributes contributes to your development, while simultaneously allowing for your values to positively affect theirs. This is the power of a relationship. Taking, giving and learning to accept all of the beauty in between.

I reflected on connecting with the core of my essence to discover what my three values were, and in a moment of insight, they revealed themselves: decency in actions, respect for philosophical and spiritual beliefs, and the desire to create a family in the future. For me, nothing was more important than that first value, that before everything else one should strive to be a good, solid and caring being. This beautifully flows into the second ideal of knowing how to endlessly accept others and their beliefs, thus revealing true respect for all. Finally, the genuine desire to create a family, to create a higher playing field of love for something that you created together. Getting in touch with these values was the first step I took to begin the process of loving myself again. I became committed to this collective essence and was ready to share my fruit with another. For the first time, I entirely believed that I would find the right person.

Luckily for me, as soon as I got back in the game, I was set up with my future wife, Dani. Every time we met, I became more intrigued by her character. Beyond her genuine care for her family and acceptance for all, I was blown away by her simplicity and authenticity. She held the ability to simply see things for what they are and always remained true to herself. I naturally grew into loving her and after a year and a half of countless lessons and exercising acceptance, I decided to propose and make her my royal Queen.

Through our marriage today, I am still learning all about relationships. Movies, media and other social platforms portray this unifying foundation as a dream-like state in which both parties are madly in love, as they drive into the eternal sunset to live happily ever after. But in all honesty, it is a job. You physically sign a contract that has no expiry date or renewals, requiring you to stay committed to one person for the remainder of your days. Your joint success requires self-awareness, diligence, empathy and above all, the willingness for each party to sacrifice their 'me' for 'we'.

Strengthening your 'we' entails working hard for one another, adopting an empathic stance and making the necessary sacrifices. Like all couples, we too have our challenges at times with broken communication and mismatched expectations, but such an approach has taught us what true companionship really is. It is not about when things are easy and fun like some fabricated episode of 'The Bachelor', but rather it is about being there, watching out for one another and defeating the obstacles faced hand in hand. It is an endless commitment, that even when days are filled with clouds of doubt and remorse, that your partner will be your umbrella to get you through the storm.

But as those clouds part, it allows for down time to be all the more enjoyable and pleasant. After six months of marriage, we finally had the privilege to take a holiday break. We decided to spend our savings and the remainder of our wedding gifts on a luxurious honeymoon; an unbelievable package trip to Barcelona, where we would embark on a seven-night cruise through three different Italian cities and the French Riviera. Having never traveled out of the country together, we were excited to take a break, enjoy the views and discover each other in new ways.

We would board The Norwegian Epic, the world's third-largest ship as of 2010, spanning over one thousand feet long and hosting over six thousand passengers. This was a floating city of restaurants, water slides, rock climbing walls, swimming pools, gyms, a performing arts theater, night clubs, a casino, bowling alleys, bars and more than one's imagination can capture. We boarded in honeymoon mode and explored the powerful vessel as if we were tourists on a different planet observing never before seen colors, shapes, tastes and smells.

Upon the second day, we woke up late and decided to go straight for the deluxe lunch buffet on the pool deck. As we exited the elevator towards the buffet, we immediately became skeptical as the dining hall was empty. To our surprise, we were sure it would be at full capacity and that we would have to hunt for vacant tables. We filled our plates with visually stunning and mouth watering delicacies, as we went in search for a table near the pool and under the sun.

As we exited the cool air-conditioned dining hall towards the deck, we discovered even more deserted tables, but found that the pool area was heavily crowded. There were at least five hundred people standing and cheering around the dance floor. Everybody seemed to be really intrigued and entertained about something that was going down. Dani and I disregarded it, as we refocused our attention to the heavenly feast before us.

Suddenly, a booming Latino accent radiated through the DJ's speakers. "Ladies and gentlemen, it's time! Welcome to the 2016 Mr. Sexy Legs Competition! We're looking for some handsome fellas who think they've got the sexiest legs on the ship. Come show us what you've got!" As the voice turned into an ambient mumble, I turned my focus back to devouring my food.

The crowd behind us was exploding with cheers and laughter. Suddenly, Dani turned towards me with a daringly devious grin on her face. "Hey Doron, I bet you don't have the balls to get up there and strut your stuff in front of all those people!"

I tried to play it cool as if her challenge was nothing but a walk in the park. "No biggie." I responded nonchalantly. "I've done crazier things."

Again the insidious grin proposed itself. A heavy moment of silence fell between us, as she was about to call my bluff. "I dare you to get up in front of all those people and join that competition!"

I swallowed my pride along with my food, as I could hear the MC screaming into his microphone, "Come on, shake it, shake it! Oh my God!" The voice again became ambient. I reflected inwards, thinking whether or not I was really capable of doing this. Despite feeling anxious, this act did not deviate from my three core beliefs. By now, I was a tree that had plenty of water and was easily able to give fruit. My attention refocused towards Dani.

"I'm game. Grab my camera. Watch this!" I declared with a tone of phony confidence. I silently prayed in my heart that Dani would stop me as we approached the dance floor.

Dani and I made our way through the crowd towards the central stage. My heart pounded stronger and stronger as we approached the open floor. The MC was in the middle of the stage rallying on the competitor to prance along the cat walk of judges. They were three middle-aged women and an elderly woman with dyed blonde hair and orange skin (probably from the amount of time she had spent under the Mediterranean sun). They seemed to be having the time of their lives! The competitor in the center was fully clothed, wearing shorts that he slightly hiked up to let the judges see the tan line on his thigh. The audience was going nuts! And in a sudden burst of insight, I began to develop a plan.

I forced myself into the end of the line of competitors as I would be the last to perform. I focused my breathing in an attempt to keep my cool, as I sweat profusely through my soul. This was it! The overly spirited MC approached me. "All right ladies and gentleman, we've got one more contestant here." I waved, not saying a word. The crowd felt bored by my timid presence. "All right judges, we have Mr. Israel over here, take it away." I dragged my feet into the heart of the sun-baked dance floor, keeping my back to the judges. I stood idle for a moment and exhaled.

Within in a blink of an eye and no warning, I jumped right out of my shorts (literally)! I kicked them off to the side, and stripped off my T-shirt like an exotic dancer grinding for an extra tip. I stood alone engulfed by the massive crowd wearing nothing but my hiked-up undies, providing a view that no man, woman or child should have to see. I shimmied my chest like Ricky Martin, shook my hips like Shakira and flexed my legs as if I was competing for the title of Mr. Universe. The audience roared with whistles, applause and laughter as Dani's stood in shock behind the camera. The MC erupted into his microphone, "Oh my God! Israel is on fire!" I made my way to the judges attempting to make them slightly uncomfortable. Of all the judges, the grandmother became most excited as she unexpectedly spanked me. The amusement level of the audience skyrocketed.

I kept on my boogie for another whole minute as the crowd buoyantly encouraged me to continue until I took a humbly bootylicious bow. I immediately clothed myself as if nothing had happened. I walked up to Dani. "Well?" She was speechless – bewildered by what just happened.

All the competitors were asked to return to the floor to declare the winner. "Ladies and gentleman, give it up for all of our contestants." We were accepted by them as their modern-day booty shaking gladiators on this floating Coliseum. "The 2016 Norwegian Epic, Mr. Sexy Legs Competition winner is… Israel!" I proudly accepted my over-glorified plastic trophy and raised it to the air. I was showered by high fives and hugs from the ships' guests as if I had just been chosen as the MVP (Most Valuable Passenger).

I returned to Dani as we laughed until our abdominals cramped. As the crowd dispersed, the elderly judge approached us. She was shorter than I thought and shared with us a smile that emanated sincere affection. "Come here, love!" She said with a well-founded, high-pitched British accent. "That was phenomenal! Absolutely spectacular!" She opened her arms and showered Dani and I with kisses, imprinting cherry red lipstick stains on our cheeks. "You are truly something special. The both of you!" Dani and I were unprepared for this strangers love.

"Thank you so much. I'm sorry, I missed your name?" I asked with a smile.

"Of course love. My name is Gwen, but you can call me Grandma. And as soon you have lots of babies, I'll be their Grandma too and send lots of gifts!" Dani and I laughed, convinced that she was surely intoxicated. However, as she lovingly looked at us, we could tell the sincerity of her intentions by the collection of wrinkles at the shores of her crisp blue eyes.

I immediately recognized the presence of an informal British Queen. I had to ask. "What brings you here to the cruise the Mediterranean?"

She smiled and paused for a moment bringing her hands towards her center. "I recently lost my daughter. She died from pneumonia three months ago."

Dani and I were dumbfounded. Was this woman for real? Cruising the world after her daughter's death? Not knowing how to properly respond, Dani sympathetically placed her hands on the woman's shoulders. "I'm so sorry. I can't even imagine what you went through." Dani said.

"Thank you dear." She sighed. "Unfortunately, slightly after that I also lost my life partner and lover of twenty years, Bob." We were in shock! "My first husband was a rancid bastard, but Bob was the love of my life and completed me. I miss him dearly." She began to tear up while holding a smile, as she grabbed onto both Dani's hands and mine. "Now I'm here traveling the world with my other daughter, just fully celebrating the spirit of life." Her tone shifted up to a higher gear. "You know, life can be a real bitch! But if you've got each other's love, you've got everything. Truly." She paused to exhale as her tears turned into kind waterfalls of wisdom. "Hold on to each other. Always love, love, love." She then jokingly pulled me in closer and whispered in my ear, "And if you break her heart, I'll bloody kill ya!'"

The three of us hysterically broke into a unique mixture of laughter, tears and enlightened thought. What originally started as a dare that challenged at what level I could share my fruit, led both Dani and I to meeting a master of love and life, who profoundly changed us forever.

Your Best Friend, the Gardener

"How are you doing?" When was the last time you looked in the mirror and lovingly asked yourself this question? I mean, asked it with the identical intention that your best friend would ask you when you feel emotionally lost? Throughout our lives, we search for friends on Facebook, followers on Instagram and more people to love us, all the while decreasing our self-love. Having become so reliant on such external validation, we almost no longer give ourselves the legitimacy to win in our own skin. But when we reflect and love inwards, we begin the process of becoming our own best friend.

Only then can you care for yourself as you would for a loved one. You will develop the confidence to transparently place yourself in front of the world without fear of losing any elements of your identity. Booty shaking challenges will be accepted with a smile, because you know that however embarrassing it is, your best friend (you) will still love you. Furthermore, you will treat yourself with sincere kindness, because that is the respect and love your best friend deserves. If we manage to so successfully deliver this love to others, then it is imperative that we serve this to ourselves.

However, there are times when we lack the knowledge, skills or attributes to provide answers. As learning beings, we should strive to make our next best friend our life partner; someone who completes us and provides a platform for meaning, rather than a reflection of our personality. A winning team does not consist of players with the exact same skill set. They are part of a diverse group that compliment each other's abilities, pushing one another to be better. Therefore, victory and relational homeostasis are achieved via the deliverance of purpose and essence to our significant other, all the while absorbing from theirs.

As mentioned above, "A tree that does not receive water cannot give any fruit." We all want to deliver our fruit to the world and doing so firstly requires becoming our own best friend. The next step then is to find that perfect gardener that will continuously cultivate your tree to help it beautifully blossom. The beauty of this greenhouse effect is that as your tree is tended to by others, you have the equal opportunity and responsibility to tend to theirs, creating a synergetic love that will drive to success.

I am humbled and thankful for my gardening Queen, and sincerely pray that you will find yours.

Royal Food for Thought

- What can you do to be a greater source of water for yourself in order to share your fruit with others?

- What attributes do you love about your best friend? Reflect upon yourself and recognize which of these attributes you possess.

Accepting the 3TMB

Throughout our lives, we find ourselves declaring statements such as, "I want my partner to be..." or "I want my job to have..." And although I agree with the endless published content on the power of visualizing what we want, this only becomes relevant when we can accept a more substantial premise; we do not always know what is best for us. We force ourselves onto the path of expectancy thinking we know what's right for us, that we know what we deserve. But ultimately, we are forfeiting chances to explore new fronts and discover new passions. Any deviation fills us with anxiety and stress, and I hate to burst your bubble, but life plans on delivering us undesired circumstances relentlessly. With that said, my intention is not that you directly interpret the word 'accept' as 'succumb,' rather, that you recognize that you have been gifted with divine conditions that will turn into opportunities for you to grow and learn from. This is the process of moving from 'expecting' to 'accepting'.

The expectations we set for others to fill are perilous potholes, which will leave a dangerous path behind for our partner to follow. When these craters are not filled we experience personal and relational turbulence that hinders our development. But when accepting, the sail is smooth as together you understand that all challenges are hidden gifts of growth, which will greatly serve you both.

As you become more willing to accept the attributes of another, do not forget that you have firstly sworn an allegiance to yourself as your own best friend. Therefore, dedicate the time to recognize your three that must be (3TMB). What are the three values that you will not bend on? I am referring to the three ideals that define you as a person, that without them, you cannot exist. Understand that these foundations should not be perceived as a lack of acceptance, but simply as self-awareness. By appreciating and staying committed to your 3TMB, you sustain an honest and loving relationship towards both yourself and your partner. Your 3TMB will keep you connected to your essence, then teach you to accept the limitless lessons that you can benefit from your companion.

As you discover new ways that your partner answers your 3TMB and you answer theirs, observe as your trees grow into a dense synergetic forest. Human nature works in a way that when our needs are answered, we wish to contribute so much more. Answer your needs, accept all as perfect and hopefully with your new life partner, endlessly contribute to each other and the world.

Royal Food for Thought

- What expectations have you set in your life that turn into obstacles?
- Define the word "accept" in your life.
- Separate yourself from everything happening around you. Connect to your essence, analyze your needs and write down: what is your 3TMB for a healthy relationship?

Integrity vs. Despair

Gwen was a British Queen who unknowingly mastered famed psychologist's Erik Erikson's final stage of psychosocial development, Integrity vs. Despair (1959). Erikson, a former prized student of

Sigmund Freud, assumed that people undergo a series of eight conflicting crises during their lifetime. These crises occur between; the psychological needs of an individual and the needs of society. Successful completion of each stage results in the development of a healthy personality, leading to the acquisition of basic virtues that serve individuals throughout their lives. Failure, however, will result in a reduced ability and a weaker sense of self.

The final of these eight stages is referred to as "Integrity vs. Despair," which generally begins from the age of sixty-five until the time of death. It focuses on the virtue of life wisdom and reflection. In the final years of one's life, the individual runs through a personal highlight reel from their earliest memory to their current state, and are then faced with a challenging closing question. "Did I live a meaningful life?" They go through a deep process of introspection, analyzing whether they have attained a sense of fulfillment and integrity, or if they painfully hold regret and despair as a result of their lack of trying. Looking back with integrity allows the person to gain the virtue of wisdom which Erikson defined as, "Informed and detached concern with life itself, even in the face of death." This is the ultimate peace of mind one can achieve.

Gwen mastered integrity, and was well aware of it. Despite facing hardships having to consecutively bury both a child and loved one, she achieved humble wisdom and pure integrity. Each of her interactions hold enlightened appreciations which she masterfully shares with others. She is driven to share these lessons of love and the power it has when given selflessly and as trivial as this may seem, there is no greater wisdom than applying this knowledge.

Observing such brilliance in her application of this has allowed me to redirect Erikson's theory to a more personal and practical level. Rather than wait for my final days to calculate my integrity vs. despair, I decided to make this a daily practice. In each day's final moments, I ask, "Did I live today with integrity or despair? Did I live today meaningfully where I positively influenced at least one person? If I left the world today, right now, could I do so peacefully, filled with integrity and wisdom?"

I believe if we each strive to complete our days with just a bit more integrity than despair, we will strive to share the same genuine love that Gwen has shared with each of us. Every connection will be a meaningful one and every moment will hold essential values. With that said, I guess that living a powerful and meaningful life begins by working from the end, then looking forward to what I wish to achieve and leave behind. That is the power of a royal legacy!

Royal Food for Thought

- What daily act can you incorporate to increase your daily integrity?
- If you were to part from this world now, how would you reflect on your life; with integrity or despair?
- What will you do, to empower the legacy that you will leave behind?

THE CROWNING OF THE STUDIOUS KING

"Make today both the first and last day of your life, and live like a King."
-DORON MAMAN

Today I sat down at an old rundown bakery located in the emptiest part of a city I am not familiar with. I scheduled to meet with a friend who lives in the area for dinner, but he was running late, so I decided to order a coffee and work on this final chapter that I wished to deliver you. As I sat on a flimsy plastic chair with a lukewarm beverage in my hand, I found myself struggling to find the right words. I was completely lost. How do I summarize so many powerful lessons? What final message do I share about all the magnificent Kings and Queens whom I have feasted with? What words can I put down that will inspire action on your behalf?

And then it hit me! A wave of inspiration providing direction proposed itself and I began to write effortlessly. Without hesitation, I put my noise-canceling headphones over my ears, blocking myself from potential distractions and successfully hit my writing rhythm. I was in a pure state of flow. After completing my second page I received a call from Daniel telling me about a new pub that might want to work with us. I spoke out loud in English over the phone for about six minutes, discussing the pros and cons of working with the new owner. But I was so excited about completing the book, I hurried the conversation to an end. "I'll have to call you back. I'm in the middle of something extremely important."

I returned to my computer to reread aloud the last sentence I wrote. "'Breakfast with Kings' is more than just a philosophy, it is a…"

Unexpectedly, my train of thought was suddenly interrupted by a surprise guest. "Were you speaking English?" A large man with short hair and coffee colored skin asked me in Hebrew. He looked to be in his early forties and was dressed warmly for the chilled night.

"Yes, I was." I wanted to finish the conversation as fast as possible to get back to my writing tempo.

"Are you American? What did you think of the recent elections?" The man was hungry for conversation and I was craving to write.

I paused for a moment to have an internal mental board meeting to decide whether I should engage in discussion or not. My mind screamed, *Doron, get back to work! You don't know this guy, you don't owe him anything. You're in the zone right now. Write!*

As my eyes shifted focus back to my keyboard for a moment, I heard a softer voice come from my heart asking, *What is this book really about? Writing, or discovering and sharing the hidden gems of people and their essences, while developing yours?*

I quietly closed my laptop and pulled off my headphones. "I was born and raised in San Diego." I said with a genuine smile. "And to tell you the truth, I don't know much about politics to have a real opinion. But I can tell you about other things I know."

The conversation gained traction as we openly spoke about the rival soccer teams we supported, different lessons we took from attempted business ventures and what our core beliefs as people are. I still did not know this stranger's name, but I was intrigued as I wished to discover what value this King could provide me.

Suddenly, the flow of our discussion came to a halt as we were interrupted by a young teenager who unexpectedly rolled in on his electric bike and sat at our table without invitation. I did not make much of it, until the stranger placed his hand on his right thigh. "This is my son," he said.

Honored to meet the young Prince, I extended my hand and curiously asked, "What's your name?"

"My name?" The young skinny boy replied while stroking his chin. "Right now, I'm…" he paused for about five-seconds. "Ohad. Right now, I'm Ohad."

Thrown off by his intermediate delay, I finally shook his hand and jokingly responded, "Great to meet you, Ohad. Right now, I'm Doron, but sometimes I'm Turbo." He chuckled.

The boy's focus immediately turned over to his father. "Dad, I want Bamba (peanut butter puffs) and Coke."

"We talked about this. You can't be putting that garbage in your body," the father claimed authoritatively.

"I know, but I really feel like having it." The boy begged.

As I was in my own journey to discover how to become royal, I decided to bravely interject. "Tell me Ohad, have you ever read the ingredients on the back of a Bamba bag?"

Again he held a prolonged pause. "Nope."

"Is there any chance that you can go get one for me?" I kindly asked.

He stood up and jumped on his bike. "I'll be back in a minute!" He rode off hard as if he was competing in the Tour de France.

As he rode away, his father cautiously leaned in towards me. "Did you notice anything strange about him?"

The unexpected question threw me off guard. "What do you mean?" I asked.

"He has autism." The father replied.

The delayed responses began to make more sense. I was not really sure what was the appropriate response, so I maintained empathic eye contact and remained silent, waiting for the father to continue. "He's the sweetest boy, and we love him dearly. He's got a heart the size of a stadium." I grew more compassionate as the father changed subjects. "But as you can see, he loves eating junk, especially Bamba and Coke. We can't get him to stop eating it! We've even taken him to therapists and psychologists over the years, but nothing's really worked." The nameless father paused to reflect and without preparation decided to extend a challenging invitation. "You seem like a smart guy. Why don't you give it a shot?"

As the fresh proposal awaited my response, I thought to myself, *I don't know much about this stuff. I'm no consultant or therapist.* But as I reflected on what was happening, the opportunity became clear: I was just delivered my official, royal invitation to become a King. I could become the influential stranger who strives to share his essence, possibly leaving someone better than before. I was game. "I'd love to!" I said with a smile.

I shook hands with the father as the boy returned with a bag of Bamba in his hand. "Here you go, Turbo," he said with a grin.

He tossed the bag into my lap. I held it with two hands and took a moment to reflect on my internal resources at my disposal. I thought of all the glorious Kings and Queens throughout my life and the lessons they shared with me. I absorbed energy from each of my life experiences believing they had served me perfectly to deliver my absolute best. I inhaled gratitude for the opportunity and exhaled my commitment to the present moment. I was going to deliver him my one hundred percent of Doron 'Turbo' Maman.

I locked eyes with the young man. "Tell me, Ohad. In your opinion, what's the world's greatest car?"

"Hmm…" Again the delayed pause. "I'd say, a Jeep Grand Cherokee."

I expected to hear something a bit more extravagant, until the father replied, "Like daddy's car."

"Exactly!" He responded nodding in agreement.

Now I was starting to see his heart. "That's a great car! If you had your own Jeep Grand Cherokee, you'd want it to be in tip-top shape, correct?"

He squinted his eyes and again nodded in agreement. "Yes. Yes, I would."

"You'd want it to take you places to discover new things so you could have exhilarating adventures, right?"

Again the relentless nod. "Yes, I would."

"I'm also sure you would take the very best care of it. Cleaning it, taking it to yearly check-ups and feeding it the best fuel possible."

"Of course!" He said enthusiastically.

I smiled. "Well, what if I told you that the Jeep is actually your body and spirit. Their combination is equivalent to the most luxurious car and it is your responsibility to take the very best care of it. If you do, it'll take you to exciting destinations in life and also help you care for the people you love, like your parents, who so dearly love you. The longer that car lasts, the more you can show your love to your friends and parents, taking them to the coolest places. But if you fill it with crummy fuel, you're going to decrease its lifetime. Do you feel me bro?" I asked with the doors to my heart wide open.

The father gawked upon the two of us as Ohad remained fully present in the conversation. "I see what you're saying," he replied while leaning in.

"I've only known you for a short while, but you seem to me like a smart man. You wouldn't fill up with fuel that people use to clean their toilets (Coke), or with processed foods containing unknown chemicals (Bamba), right? You'd only put in the finest fuel because you want your car to return the relentless love you've been gifted with by your parents, for as long as possible and to as many people as possible."

His dark brown eyes looked deep into mine as I felt I my official crowning as a King coming. "I love my father and mother. I want to give them everything," he replied. The father held back his breath as he silently wiped his running tears.

Although I knew I had him hooked, I wanted to leave him with a final powerful incentive. "Let's make a deal." I placed the bag of Bamba on the table in front of him. "If you promise me to never eat and drink this junk again, I swear to you that I will never touch those contaminated fuels as well. This means that if you stay healthy and deliver your naturally-energized love to all those in your life, I'll now have to live up to that same commitment. But if you give in, you'll not only hurt the people you love and influence in your life, but you'll also be distancing me from mine. I'm now dependent on you and totally trust you, because I know you'll make the right decision for your loved ones and for mine." I extended my hand over the peanut treat. "Do we have a deal?"

The unnamed father gulped aloud as we all felt the presence of something special about to happen. Ohad stroked his chin one final time and without hesitation confidently replied, "Deal." He threw the bag of Bamba into a dark corner and embraced me with a royal hug that sent shockwaves through my soul. He then innocently asked his father, "Can I please have some money to buy a bottle of water?"

The father gently smiled, giving him some change to go and buy the beverage. "I've never seen anything like that," the father claimed in awe. "Who are you?"

I smiled with my eyes down feeling both extreme gratitude and humility for the present moment. "Just a man learning to become a King. Thank you for the chance to talk to your son."

The father and I exchanged a few more words and our personal information to stay in touch. Since then, I have not touched either of those contaminated fuels and plan continuing to stay true to my word, believing that Ohad is staying true to his.

I left the bakery that night having experienced an emotional high like never before. Never would I have thought that these would be the grounds upon which I would be crowned. Never had I shared a discussion where I was so fully devoted to giving another my all. Never had I been privileged by a stranger to so openly come into their heart.

And now I write to you as a humble and studious King; someone who is in a never-ending pursuit of attaining and delivering values while striving to inspire action and meaning in others. I search daily for Kings and Queens with whom to share royal meals; the kind of meals that nutritiously feed my soul, thereby giving me the strength to feed others. This never-ending cycle has only resulted in growth and contribution and there is no higher calling in this world.

As I have done with all the highnesses mentioned in this book, I wish to share with you my final three takeaways as the studious King I've become and am still becoming. I wish to connect you to my essence, the part of my heart that I seek to deliver daily. I am deeply humbled that you have chosen to read my memoirs and reflect upon my understandings. I hope that we too can one day share a royal meal, feasting on values which will fill our hearts with ideals and our days with meaning, so please reach out to me by any means possible.

I deliver these final gifts to you with my greatest love and deepest respect. I will see you at breakfast.

Don't Look Down, Look Around

Our eyes are glued to digital screens. We spend ten hours a day on average staring at computers, televisions and smartphones as there seems to be a spreading epidemic of FOMO (Fear of Missing Out) syndrome. We need our online fix of daily gossip, we want instant news updates and fear being tagged as 'uninformed', thereby leaving us no choice but to bow down to the mentality of the dominating matrix.

And with that said, it breaks my heart because everywhere I look, there are always people who are mentally enslaved to their gadgets and circumstances! People go out on dates spending more time looking at their phones than they do observing the eye color of their companion. Families share quality time facing their television sets rather than facing one another. Even when I ride the train, I sit next to unknown remarkable Kings and Queens and see everybody retreat into their own technological turtle shell. What about the FOMO on connecting with amazing people? Is this not the real FOMO syndrome we should be experiencing?

As the surrounding paradigm tempted me with its desirable inclination to drive my gaze back into my computer screen, I recognized that I may be missing the opportunity to connect to true royalty. Therefore, I closed my laptop and decided to no longer look down, but rather, look around. Why should I have my face illuminated by a device, when I can have my soul illuminated by talking to the stranger seated next to me? If we became as committed to our face-to-face conversations as we are to our devices, we would endlessly discover remarkable lessons.

For many years, my friends have joked that the stories such as the ones I have shared are only things that seem to happen to me. But, the odds of this happening to you are identical, the only difference is that rather than looking down, I am looking around. I spend less time looking down at my technological devices and more time looking around for natural inspiration. I do not look down, sulking in my failed endeavors. Rather I look around for what opportunities they have created. When a young Prince like Ohad and his father present themselves before me, I do not look down, removing myself from the scenario. Instead, I look around to see what can I do to step up as a fellow human being to make this unexpected relationship that much more powerful and impactful.

At the beginning of the book, I shared with you my 'funeral psychology' reflecting how we should each live with such meaning that we gain new participants to attend our final parting each day. But now, I understand that the true underlying humility of this mindset is in how we connect with others, as if tomorrow is to be not just our burial, but their burial as well. If we conduct our conversations with people as if it were our last opportunity to connect with them, we would more often drink from their fountain of wisdom, create timeless memories and most importantly, recognize and appreciate all they've given. Looking around teaches us to provide others with transcendent respect, while learning how to live a more impactful life in the future.

Royal Food for Thought

- Spend the day looking around rather than just looking down. What new treasure did you discover in yourself? What royal value did you discover in another?

- Take the opportunity to treat your next conversation with a loved one as if it were your last. What will you take from them? What will you acknowledge them with?

Deliver Your Essence

Wake up! You have just been graciously granted twenty-four hours to go out and create something phenomenal that will serve yourself and others for years to come. Do you even get how many life forces at this moment would kill to be in your position? You could have been so many different things. You could have been a tree, or a car, or one of the rejected sperm cells that did not make it into your mother's eggs. Yet here you are, and you beat those billions of other cells, and I believe there must be a reason for that. And now you are here with a fully functional brain and soul, reading this book, connecting to genuinely sincere values. So what are you going to do today to share your gifts?

Over the course of your life, family, friends and even haters have invested time into you, all with the (direct or indirect) goal of helping you discover and create your own authentic brand that will serve others. This is your essence, your greatest possession. Does it not blow you away that there have been over one hundred billion people that have walked this earth, but you are the only of your kind? Never has there or will there be another person like you who has had your experiences and understandings. This means that only you can contribute to others all that you have been privileged to learn as a King or Queen.

My experience with Ohad helped me realize that if I do not share the abundantly impressive lessons that I have been taught, then my life is meaningless. If I do not look for and take advantage of opportunities to deliver my essence to better the quality of the lives of others, I may as well have been something else in this world. If I am alive, it is my responsibility to fully commit to the person in front of me and in addition to learning from them, to find a way to place my personally-branded value in their heart so they can live a greater life.

Let me be clear, I was not striving to rehabilitate Ohad from downing bottles of carbonated sugars or constantly snacking on various contaminated fuels. I was on a mission to deliver a message to both Ohad and his father, that even a complete stranger in the emptiest part of an estranged city, in the place you would least expect, can extend love and genuine care. Whether they remember me or attend my funeral is irrelevant as I believe that this message will stay in their hearts for years to come, and hopefully they will find their way to deliver it to others. Maybe even to you.

So wake up! Open your eyes and see what amazing chances you have been gifted with to deliver your essence. Appreciate that some lucky person that you have never met will potentially have their lives changed forever by you, just because you decided to care. Treat this average day as if it were your last, imprint meaning on all you come in contact with and leave an epic path for others to follow.

Royal Food for Thought

- What is the core value of your essence? What is the unique gift that you will contribute to all you touch?
- Think of three new ways that you can deliver your essence that will imprint your signature on their heart for years to come.

Breakfast with Kings

Breakfast with Kings is more than just a philosophy. It is a practical way of life that masterfully balances between being both a humble emperor of meaning and an inquisitive student of curiosity. It has granted me so many beautiful appreciations that have truly humbled me, along with shifting my train of thought to an endlessly grateful one.

Practically speaking, beyond my daily interactions and spontaneous adventures, I have transformed this approach into a weekly routine. Almost every Friday, I meet for a worthy breakfast with my four dearest friends, each of whom provides me values of the highest royal standards. We meet at the local boutique coffee shop in the city we grew up in, filling our stomachs with delicious assortments, then sharing equally appetizing discussions to replenish our souls. It is the kind of meal that you can feel the shared synergetic experience which greatly exceeds the taste of the already heavenly food. It is truly something magical, and no matter how much I eat, I always find myself hungry for more.

As I sit with these Kings, I realize that beyond the praised iconic business moguls, the phenomenal star athletes and glamorously attractive celebrities, there are infinite unnoticed heroes who contribute enormous value on a daily basis. I am talking about the on-campus security guard who greets you with a smile each morning, the stranger who high fives you during your evening run or even the person across the street who picks up a piece of trash that is not hers, thinking nobody is watching.

So pause. Take the moment to acknowledge them. Let them know, that their simple act and determination to deliver their heart, places them at a status of royalty. Help them break their spiritual fast by recognizing the contribution of their actions which they might believe others have overlooked. I know that such openness can be hard. If someone were to come up to me randomly and say, "Hey Doron, there's no special reason that I'm telling you this, but I just want you to know that I'm so thankful for all you've given." I too might initially respond with suspicion. However, I guarantee that I will become that much more driven to give my heart to others as I have to that person, and hopefully so will you.

I invite you to get REAL. Recognize, Encourage, Appreciate and Love the Kings and Queens in your life. Invite them to your own 'Breakfast with Kings' and have them sit nobly at your table as you share profound understandings that will spill over into the other realms of your life. This is your chance to make everyday both the first and last day of your life. The first as a student, as if you are learning and absorbing great wisdom from the people around you for the first time. And the last day as a King or Queen, as if it were your final opportunity to contribute to them your essence. Bon appétit.

Royal Food for Thought

- Invite your closest friends to your own 'Breakfast with Kings'. Share with them a delicious meal comprised of great food and meaningful discussions. What was your main takeaway from each King and Queen? What did you bestow onto them?

- Choose a person in your life that is not fully aware of your appreciation for them. It can be a parent, friend or complete stranger. Sit with them face-to-face and say the following: "Everything is okay, there's no need to worry. It was just really important for me to tell you that __________ and for that, I am thankful." Fill in that blank, and share from your heart what you have taken from them as a King or Queen and how it has inspired you.

- How has this changed your relationship with the person?